I've Got It!

Pre-Algebra Skills

Easy-to-Use Assessments to Show Proof of Mastery

by Marjorie Frank
and Jill Norris

Incentive Publications, Inc.
Nashville, Tennessee

Illustrated by Kathleen Bullock
Cover by Geoffrey Brittingham
Edited by Stephanie McGuirk
Math edited by Scott Norris and K. Noel Frietas

ISBN 978-0-86530-524-3

Copyright ©2008 by Incentive Publications, Inc., Nashville, TN. All rights reserved. No part of this publication may be reproduced, stored in a retrieval system, or transmitted in any form or by any means (electronic, mechanical, photocopying, recording, or otherwise) without written permission from Incentive Publications, Inc., with the exception below.

Pages labeled with the statement **©2008 by Incentive Publications, Inc., Nashville, TN** are intended for reproduction. Permission is hereby granted to the purchaser of one copy of **I'VE GOT IT! — PRE-ALGEBRA SKILLS** to reproduce these pages in sufficient quantities for meeting the purchaser's own classroom needs only.

1 2 3 4 5 6 7 8 9 10   11 10 09 08

PRINTED IN THE UNITED STATES OF AMERICA
www.incentivepublications.com

Table of Contents

page

What Do You Need to Know at the End of This Course? *(Introduction)*

    To the Student 5

    To the Teacher 6

An Overview of Pre-Algebra, Grades 7, 8, and 9 7
(Thirty-five End-of-Course Skills Broken into Specific Tasks)

Task Pages

Task 1	Recognize and define numbers and number systems.	a 14 b 15
Task 2	Compare and order numbers.	a 16 b 17
Task 3	Recognize and use properties of numbers and operations.	a 18 b 19
Task 4	Recognize and use order of operations.	a 20 b 21
Task 5	Perform operations with positive and negative numbers.	a 22 b 23
Task 6	Identify elements of mathematical expressions.	a 24 b 25
Task 7	Read and write expressions.	a 26 b 27
Task 8	Simplify and evaluate expressions.	a 28 b 29
Task 9	Evaluate expressions with radicals and exponents.	a 30 b 31
Task 10	Perform operations with radicals and exponents.	a 32 b 33
Task 11	Recognize and use factors and multiples.	a 34 b 35
Task 12	Perform operations with fractions and decimals.	a 36 b 37
Task 13	Solve problems with percent.	a 38 b 39
Task 14	Factor expressions and equations.	a 40 b 41
Task 15	Translate problems into equations.	a 42 b 43

Task 16	Solve equations using inverse operations.	a 44	b 45
Task 17	Solve equations with one variable and one step.	a 46	b 47
Task 18	Solve multi-step equations.	a 48	b 49
Task 19	Solve equations with rational numbers.	a 50	b 51
Task 20	Solve equations with radicals and exponents.	a 52	b 53
Task 21	Find rate, time, and distance.	a 54	b 55
Task 22	Solve problems with ratio and proportion.	a 56	b 57
Task 23	Use ratios to show probability.	a 58	b 59
Task 24	Write, solve, and graph inequalities.	a 60	b 61
Task 25	Solve equations with more than one variable.	a 62	b 63
Task 26	Compare geometric figures.	a 64	b 65
Task 27	Use formulas to find area and volume of figures.	a 66	b 67
Task 28	Recognize and use relationships in right triangles.	a 68	b 69
Task 29	Graph number pairs on a coordinate grid.	a 70	b 71
Task 30	Plot transformations of figures on a grid.	a 72	b 73
Task 31	Identify and describe functions.	a 74	b 75
Task 32	Identify and graph linear equations.	a 76	b 77
Task 33	Determine features of linear equations.	a 78	b 79
Task 34	Identify and operate with polynomials.	a 80	b 81
Task 35	Use algebra to solve a variety of problems.	a 82	b 83

Student Record Sheet for Pre-Algebra End-of-Course Tasks 84

Class Record Sheet for Pre-Algebra End-of-Course Tasks 85

Putting It All Together (A Cumulative Checkup) 86

Answer Key 92

What Do You Need to Know at the End of This Course?

To the student . . .

You're taking a class that includes pre-algebra skills in areas such as number systems and properties, operations with real numbers, integers, mathematical expressions, equations, geometric formulas, factoring, radical and exponential numbers, ratio, proportion, functions, linear equations, graphing, and using algebraic concepts in problem solving. So, how do you know when you've got these? This book will show you. It gives details of what you need to know and be able to do to have mastered the basic skills for a pre-algebra course.

Here's how to use the book . . . it's as easy as 1-2-3-4:

First, check out the overview of skills and tasks. *(pages 7–13)*

- Look over the 35 tasks that you should be able to do at the end of the course.
- Each task is written in the form of something you need to be able to do.
- Underneath each of the tasks is a list of specific skills or "sub"-tasks.
- These are the things that you do **to show** you know the larger task.

Complete the 35 tasks. *(pages 14–83)*

- Each task has TWO versions—**a** and **b**.
  *(This gives you **two** chances to show you can do the task.)*
- Each version has FIVE items or questions.
- Do one version. Then check your answers. If you missed any, you need to brush up on that skill. Figure out why you missed the items that you missed.
- Ask for help if you need it.
- When you feel more confident with this task, try the second version.

Fill out the record sheet. *(page 84)*

- Keep track of your accomplishments. Make a copy of this record sheet.
- Write down your score and the date for each of the tasks you do.

Put it all together with a cumulative review. *(pages 86–91)*

- This review includes all the tasks.
- Solve the problems and use all 35 skills.
- Discover the errors and make appropriate corrections.
- When you can do each of the 35 tasks and the cumulative review successfully, you'll have shown that you have a solid background in pre-algebra skills.

To the teacher . . .

You can use this book in a variety of ways to help your students show that they know what they need to know by the end of the course. Here are some suggestions . . .

- Review the course overview thoroughly. (pages 7–13)

- Provide thorough instruction and resources during the course to build students' understanding and let them practice these skills.

- When students are ready to show what they know, get them started on the 35 tasks.

- Provide more instruction when a student cannot complete all five items correctly. Discuss the right and wrong answers. Help each student get to the place where he or she is fluent with the concept and process before having the student try the second version of the task.

- Use the two versions of the end-of-course tasks
    - . . . as pretests and posttests
    - . . . as consecutive checkups (with instruction in between)
    - . . . as aids in your instruction
    - . . . at the beginning of the course and at the end of the course
    - . . . throughout the year
    - . . . any time students are ready
    - . . . with individuals or the whole group

- Encourage students to keep their own record of progress on these tasks. (See **Student Record Sheet**, page 84.)

- Keep a class record of student progress on the tasks. (See **Teacher Record Sheet**, page 85.)

- Choose an appropriate time for the cumulative review. (See **Putting It All Together**, pages 86–91.) A student may take this when he or she is ready. Or, you might give it to the entire class when you feel the timing is right.

- If a student misses more than five items on the cumulative review, identify the areas of confusion, and find a way to reteach that task.

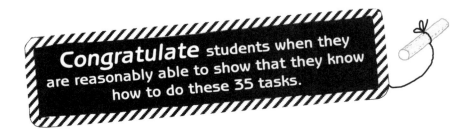

Showing Proof of Mastery

By the end of your pre-algebra course, you should be able to complete successfully the following 35 tasks. Note that each task is broken into its component skills. Showing that you have each of the skills and can complete the tasks is one way to show proof of mastery.

Task 1	**Recognize and define numbers and number systems.** *You show that you can do this task when you:* • Distinguish between different kinds of numbers and number systems. • Determine the absolute value of a number. • Determine the opposite of a number. • Identify the reciprocal of a number. • Distinguish between prime and composite numbers.
Task 2	**Compare and order numbers.** *You show that you can do this task when you:* • Compare values of different kinds of numbers. • Order numbers according to their value. • Identify different ways to express the same value. • Use <, >, or = signs to compare numbers.
Task 3	**Recognize and use properties of numbers and operations.** *You show that you can do this task when you:* • Identify and use the commutative and associative properties for addition and multiplication. • Identify and use the distributive property. • Identify and use the additive and multiplicative identity properties. • Identify and use the additive and multiplicative inverse properties. • Identify and use properties to justify individual steps in the solution of problems. • Identify and use the multiplicative property of zero.
Task 4	**Recognize and use order of operations.** *You show that you can do this task when you:* • Identify order for operations (PEMDAS). • Apply the order of operations to simplify or evaluate an expression. • Show how order of operations makes a difference in the answer. • Choose a grouping of elements to produce a specific answer.
Task 5	**Perform operations with positive and negative numbers.** *You show that you can do this task when you:* • Add positive and negative numbers. • Subtract positive and negative numbers. • Multiply positive and negative numbers. • Divide positive and negative numbers. • Solve real-life problems with positive and negative numbers.

Task 6

Identify elements of mathematical expressions.

You show that you can do this task when you:

- Identify variables in expressions and equations.
- Identify terms, like terms, and unlike terms.
- Identify coefficients of variables.
- Distinguish between expressions, equations, and inequalities.
- Distinguish between monomial, binomial, and polynomial expressions.

Task 7

Read and write expressions.

You show that you can do this task when you:

- Match words to expressions written with numbers and symbols.
- Match mathematical expressions to words.
- Write expressions to match words.
- Write words to match expressions.

Task 8

Simplify and evaluate expressions.

You show that you can do this task when you:

- Simplify expressions by combining like terms.
- Simplify expressions by evaluating individual terms.
- Simplify expressions by using properties of operations.
- Recognize simplified expressions.
- Evaluate expressions with whole numbers or rational numbers.

Task 9

Evaluate expressions with roots, radicals, and exponents.

You show that you can do this task when you:

- Evaluate and write expressions with radicals or positive exponents.
- Evaluate and write expressions with negative exponents.
- Evaluate and write expressions with fractional exponents.
- Evaluate and write expressions with scientific notation.

Task 10

Perform operations with roots, radicals, and exponents.

You show that you can do this task when you:

- Perform operations with exponential numbers.
- Perform operations with scientific notation.
- Raise a power to a power.
- Perform operations with radicals.

Task 11

Recognize and use factors and multiples.

You show that you can do this task when you:

- Determine divisibility of a number.
- Recognize factors of a number.
- Recognize multiples of a number.
- Identify common multiples, common factors, GCF, and LCM for a set of numbers.
- Recognize prime factorization of a number.
- Recognize multiples of a number.

Task 12

Perform operations with fractions and decimals.

You show that you can do this task when you:

- Perform operations with decimals.
- Simplify fractions; find common denominators.
- Add and subtract fractions and mixed numerals.
- Multiply and divide fractions and mixed numerals.
- Solve real-life problems with fractions and decimals.

Task 13

Solve problems with percent.

You show that you can do this task when you:

- Write percent as decimal or fraction; write a decimal or fraction as a percent.
- Find a percent of a number.
- Given a percent, find a base number.
- Use percent to find discounts, markup, interest, or taxes.
- Find percent of change.

Task 14

Factor expressions and equations.

You show that you can do this task when you:

- Identify factors of an expression.
- Identify prime factors of an expression.
- Factor expressions.
- Identify the greatest common factor of terms in an expression.
- Identify correctly-factored expressions.

Task 15

Translate problems into equations.

You show that you can do this task when you:

- Choose an equation that can help to solve a word problem.
- Write a word problem as an equation.
- Write equations to solve problems.
- Use equations to solve real-life problems.

Task 16

Solve equations using inverse operations.

You show that you can do this task when you:

- Use the inverse operations of addition and subtraction to solve equations.
- Use the inverse operations of multiplication and division to solve equations.

Task 17

Solve equations with one variable and one step.

You show that you can do this task when you:

- Solve one-step, one-variable equations with whole numbers.
- Solve one-step, one-variable equations with positive or negative numbers.
- Solve one-step, one-variable equations with exponents or radicals.
- Solve one-step, one-variable equations with fractions or decimals.

Task 18	**Solve multi-step equations.**
	You show that you can do this task when you:
	• Solve multi-step equations with whole numbers.
	• Solve multi-step equations with positive or negative numbers.

Task 19	**Solve equations with rational numbers.**
	You show that you can do this task when you:
	• Solve multi-step equations with fractions.
	• Solve multi-step equations with decimals.
	• Compare solutions of different equations.

Task 20	**Solve equations with radicals and exponents.**
	You show that you can do this task when you:
	• Solve multi-step equations with exponential numbers.
	• Solve multi-step equations with radicals.
	• Solve multi-step equations with scientific notation.
	• Identify correctly-solved equations with radicals and exponents.

Task 21	**Find rate, time, and distance.**
	You show that you can do this task when you:
	• Find rate, time, or distance.
	• Compare ratios.
	• Find rate per unit.
	• Solve real-life rate problems.

Task 22	**Solve problems with ratio and proportion.**
	You show that you can do this task when you:
	• Use cross-multiplication to solve proportions.
	• Write a pair of ratios to show a proportion.
	• Use ratio to show problem solutions.
	• Write a ratio in simplest form.
	• Set up proportions to solve real-life problems.

Task 23	**Use ratios to show probability.**
	You show that you can do this task when you:
	• Use a ratio to show probability of an outcome.
	• Use a ratio to show probability of two independent outcomes.
	• Use a ratio to show probability of two dependent events.
	• Use a ratio to show odds of an event.
	• Write ratios to show combinations or permutations.
	• Write a ratio to show probability in solutions of real-life problems.

Task 24

Write, solve, and graph inequalities.

You show that you can do this task when you:

- Read and write inequalities.
- Solve inequalities.
- Recognize the graph of a specific inequality.
- Create graphs of inequalities.
- Solve real-life inequality problems.

Task 25

Solve equations with more than one variable.

You show that you can do this task when you:

- Given one variable in an equation, find another.
- Find different solutions as the value of one variable changes.
- Given relationship between variables, find the value of more than one variable.

Task 26

Compare geometric figures.

You show that you can do this task when you:

- Identify similar figures.
- Identify congruent figures.
- Compare components in congruent and similar figures.
- Find measurements of corresponding elements of congruent figures.
- Use knowledge of similarity to evaluate scale drawings.

Task 27

Use formulas to find area and volume of figures.

You show that you can do this task when you:

- Find the area of plane figures.
- Find surface area of space figures.
- Find volume of space figures.
- Compare areas, surface areas, and volumes of figures.
- Manipulate formulas to find other variables.
- Use formulas to find solutions to real-life problems.

Task 28

Recognize and use relationships in right triangles.

You show that you can do this task when you:

- Identify the relationship of angles in a right triangle.
- Identify the relationship of leg lengths in a right triangle.
- Use the Pythagorean Theorem to find the length of a right triangle leg.
- Given two points on a grid, use the Pythagorean Theorem to find the distance between them.

Task 29
Graph number pairs on a coordinate grid.
You show that you can do this task when you:
- Identify the quadrants on a coordinate grid.
- Write a pair of numbers to indicate location on a grid.
- Locate a point or item on a coordinate grid.
- Plot points on a 4-quadrant grid.
- Make reasoned judgments about where points will be located.

Task 30
Plot transformations of figures on a grid.
You show that you can do this task when you:
- Recognize transformations of figures.
- Draw transformations of figures.
- Identify locations of figures or points on a figure after a flip.
- Identify locations of figures or points on a figure after a turn.
- Identify locations of figures or points on a figure after a rotation.

Task 31
Identify and describe functions.
You show that you can do this task when you:
- Define or identify functions.
- Identify a function from a graph.
- Recognize the domain and range of a function.
- Complete a function table.
- Translate points from a function table to a graph.

Task 32
Identify and graph linear equations.
You show that you can do this task when you:
- Recognize linear equations.
- Recognize graph of a specific equation.
- Identify rise and run of a line on a graph or of a line from an equation.
- Identify slope from a graph.
- Write an equation in slope-intercept form.
- Graph linear equations.

Task 33
Determine features of linear equations.
You show that you can do this task when you:
- Show understanding of slope, x-intercept, and y-intercept.
- Distinguish between positive and negative slope.
- Given two points on a line, determine slope.
- Determine y-intercept from an equation.
- Given a point on a line, and the equation of a line parallel to it, find an equation for the first line.

Task 34

Identify and operate with polynomials.

You show that you can do this task when you:

- Define and recognize monomials and polynomials.
- Evaluate polynomials.
- Simplify polynomials.
- Add and subtract polynomials.
- Use the FOIL method to multiply polynomials.
- Factor polynomials.

Task 35

Use algebra to solve a variety of problems.

You show that you can do this task when you:

- Write an equation to solve a variety of real-life problems.
- Use formulas to solve real-life problems.

Recognize and define numbers and number systems.

Do you know it? Show it:

1 Isaiah estimated that his pet toad had this number of warts: $\sqrt{289}$.
Circle the number sets to which this number belongs.

rational   irrational   real   integers   natural

2 Find
  a. the absolute value of (–7)
  b. the opposite of 12
  c. $|-7| + |4|$

3 Two frogs compete to see which one can hop to the most lily pads without stopping for a rest. The number of pads that Francis Frog manages to land on is equal to the smallest 2-digit prime number. Frederica Frog's total is the smallest 2-digit composite number.
Which frog wins the competition?

4 Write the reciprocal of each number.
  a. $1\frac{1}{2}$ _____   c. (–1) _____   e. 1 _____
  b. 8 _____   d. 4 _____   f. (–6) _____

5 Eli has finished a question on a math test. Did he get it right?
Circle the letters of any items that he answered correctly.

Write T or F to show that each statement is true or false.

_T_ a. Pi is a rational number.
_T_ b. Rational numbers are real numbers.
_T_ c. Integers are rational numbers.
_T_ d. Zero is a natural number.
_T_ e. All positive numbers are whole numbers.
_F_ f. Irrational numbers are not real numbers.
_F_ g. All fractions are rational numbers.
_F_ h. All decimals are integers.

Recognize and define numbers and number systems.

Do you know it? Show it:

1 Some frogs can leap a distance 35 times their body length. For one cricket frog, this is about 223 inches. Is this number prime or composite?

2 Circle the rational numbers.

4^{-3} $\sqrt{3}$ 2.4545   0.062 $\frac{3}{4}$ –14

π 9^2 6.2×10^3 3.16   0.110101011101 . . . . . .

3 Two of the following statements are not true. Correct them to make them true.

a. $|-9| > |6|$ c. $|12| < |-7|$ e. $|-5| > 0$

b. $|-8| - |9| = -1$ d. $|2| + |-12| = 10$ f. $|9| - |-4| = 5$

4 Write the reciprocal of each number.

a. $\frac{4}{7}$ _____   c. (-5) _____   e. $\frac{3}{4}$ _____

b. $\frac{x}{2}$ _____   d. 15 _____   f. $\sqrt{6}$ _____

---

5 Which statements are always true?

A. Natural numbers are also called counting numbers.

B. Repeating decimals are rational numbers.

C. Radicals are irrational numbers.

D. The square of a number is a positive number.

E. The root of an even number is a positive number.

F. Irrational numbers are real numbers.

G. Repeating decimals are irrational.

Compare and order numbers.

Do you know it? Show it:

1 Dr. Felix U. Jaw, dentist, gave away toothbrushes last week. On which day did Dr. Jaw give away the greatest number of toothbrushes?

Monday: $2(\sqrt{289})$ Tuesday: 2^5 Wednesday: $3(3^2)$

Thursday: 3^3 Friday: $\frac{1}{2}(4^3)$

2 Which is not true?
- ○ $-4 < (\frac{5}{10})^2$
- ○ $\sqrt{144} = 2(2^8)$
- ○ $0.606 < 0.6606$
- ○ $4^5 > (4)^{-5}$

3 What is $\frac{5}{8}$ written as a decimal?

4 Which list shows numbers in order of value from least to greatest?

a. -2^6; -4^5; 1.106; $\frac{14}{9}$; 3.15; π; 2.6×10^2; $\sqrt{169}$

b. -4^5; $\frac{14}{9}$; 1.106; π; 3.15; -2^6; $\sqrt{169}$; 2.6×10^2

c. -4^5; 1.106; $\frac{14}{9}$; π; 3.15; $\sqrt{169}$; -2^6; 2.6×10^2

d. -2^6; -4^5; 1.106; $\frac{14}{9}$; 3.15; 2.6×10^2; $\sqrt{169}$; π

5 Four friends shared information about costs of their dental work.
- The cost of Charlie's tooth extraction increased by a significant percentage over the extraction he paid for five years ago. The first one was $30. The most recent one cost $222.
- Maria has paid off all but 64 cents of her dentist bill.
- Jayde learned that her dentist had given her a discount of $32 on her bill.
- Sam just paid the last $40 of a bill for filling five cavities.

Which numbers below represent the same four values described in the information above? Circle them.

6.4×10^{-2} 64% $(-2)^5$ $\sqrt[3]{64{,}000}$ 2^6 640%

$\sqrt[2]{6400}$ 4^3 $\sqrt[3]{640}$ 6.4% 6.4×10^{-1}

What is the right time to go to the dentist?

2:30!

Compare and order numbers.

Do you know it? Show it:

1 For each example, circle the number with greatest value.

a. $\sqrt{121}$ or 3^4 or $2(2^3)$

b. $\frac{5}{9}$ or $\frac{3}{5}$ or $\frac{2}{3}$

2 Which is not true?

○ $-5 < (\frac{12}{3})^2$ ○ $0.9919 < 0.9909$

○ $\sqrt{256} = \frac{1}{2}(2^5)$ ○ $-6^3 > (-6)^{-3}$

3 Sasha wrote a check for the dentist's bill. She spent 81.2% of the money in her bank account. What is this number written as a decimal?

4 Which list shows numbers in order of value from least to greatest?

a. $\sqrt{196}$; $\frac{8}{19}$; 0.63; π; 1.3×10^2; -2^4; 12

b. $\frac{8}{19}$; 0.63; π; 12; $\sqrt{196}$; -2^4; 1.3×10^2

c. -2^4; 0.63; $\frac{8}{19}$; π; 12; $\sqrt{196}$; 1.3×10^2

d. $\frac{8}{19}$; 0.63; π; 12; -2^4; 1.3×10^2; $\sqrt{196}$

5 Dentists use a system of numbering teeth, so that they can keep track of dental conditions and work for patients. Tooth number 1 is the tooth farthest back on the right side of the mouth in the upper jaw. The numbers continue across the upper teeth and continue from left to right across the bottom jaw.

Each number below has a value to match the number of a tooth. Find the value of each number. Color the tooth that matches that number.

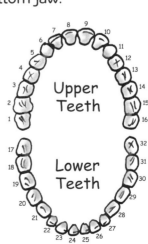

a. $\sqrt{400} - \sqrt{49}$ d. $4^2 + \sqrt{100}$

b. 2700×10^{-2} e. $|-18|$

c. $132 \div 12$ f. $\sqrt[3]{64}$

I've Got It!—Pre-Algebra Skills
Copyright ©2008 by Incentive Publications, Inc., Nashville, TN.

Use properties of numbers and operations.

Do you know it? Show it:

1. Mr. Cate's eighth grade homeroom class collected 460 plastic water bottles in January, 750 in February, and 800 in March. Ms. Lucia's class collected 750 water bottles in January, 800 in February, and 460 in March. Both classes had the same number of bottles at the end of the three months. This situation is an example of which property?

    a. associative for addition   d. commutative for addition

    b. associative for multiplication   e. commutative for multiplication

    c. distributive   f. multiplicative identity

2. Finish the statement using the distributive property.

    $n(3 + 9) =$ _____

3. Which statement best illustrates the additive identity property?

○ $5 + (-5) = 0$ ○ $x \cdot x = x^2$ ○ $25 + 1 = 26$

○ $8y \cdot 1 = 8y$ ○ $(3 \cdot 7) + 0 = 21$ ○ $(-12) + 5 = 5 + (-12)$

4. Which property is represented by the following equation?

    $(10 \cdot 6) \cdot 4 = 10 \cdot (6 \cdot 4)$

5. Review the problem solution shown. In each step where you see an empty line, identify the property that was used by the problem-solver.

Monday was a slow day for Scott's efforts to collect bottles. Solve the equation to find the average number he collected at each stop (x).

Bottle Collections: Average Per Stop

$9x - 12 = 0 + 6$

$9x - 12 = 6$ _____

$9x - 12 + 12 = 6 + 12$ _____

$9x = 18$

$\dfrac{9x}{9} = \dfrac{18}{9}$ _____

$x = 2$

Use properties of numbers and operations.

Do you know it? Show it:

1. To earn money for her basketball team, Erika gathered soda pop cans. One day she found she got five cents apiece for six groups of nine cans. The next day she got five cents apiece for six cans nine different times. The amount of money she earned was the same on both days. This situation is an example of which property?

   a. associative for addition
   b. associative for multiplication
   c. inverse operations
   d. commutative property for addition
   e. commutative for multiplication
   f. additive identity

2. Finish the statement using the distributive property.
$10(6 - 4x + 12y) =$ _____

3. Which statement best illustrates the multiplicative identity property?
   ○ $8(-1) = -8$
   ○ $g \cdot g = g^2$
   ○ $55 \cdot 1 = 55$
   ○ $3p + 0 = 3p$
   ○ $4 \cdot \frac{1}{4} = 1$
   ○ $(-6) + 4 + 0 = 4 + 0 + (-6)$

4. Which property is represented by the following equation?
$\frac{5}{6} \cdot \frac{6}{5} = 1$

5. Review the problem solution shown. In each step where you see an empty line, identify the property that was used by the problem-solver.

Jordan filled a number of large garbage bags with cans she collected. Solve the equations to find that number.

$$6(n + 4) = 49 + n$$
$$6n + 24 = 49 + n \text{ _____}$$
$$6n + 24 - 24 = 49 + n - 24 \text{ _____}$$
$$6n = 25 + n$$
$$6n - n = 25 + n - n \text{ _____}$$
$$5n = 25$$
$$\frac{5n}{5} = \frac{25}{5} \text{ _____}$$
$$n = 5$$

Recognize and use order of operations.

Do you know it? Show it:

1. Antonio's parents limit the amount of time he can spend on the phone on school nights. He is allowed one-third of the time he spends on all his homework. Last night he spent 30 minutes on science, twice as long on math, and twice as long on language as on math. The following expression represents his phone time. What operation should be done first in order to evaluate the expression?

$$\frac{30 + (2 \cdot 30) + (2 \cdot 2 \cdot 30)}{3}$$

2. Use the correct order of operations to evaluate this expression.

$$3(2 + 9) - 3 + 2^3 + 12$$

3. In evaluating this expression: $2[-1(-4 - 3) + 5] + 6^2$

What operation should be performed first?
What operation should be performed second?
What operation should be performed last?

4. Which grouping yields a solution of 100?

a. $5 \cdot (4 \cdot 6) + 3 - (8 \cdot 3^2) + 1$ c. $(5 \cdot 4) \cdot 6 + 3 - (8 \cdot 3^2) + 1$

b. $5 \cdot 4 \cdot (6 + 3) - 8(3^2 + 1)$ d. $(5 \cdot 4 \cdot 6) + 3 - (8 \cdot 3^2 + 1)$

5. On Wednesday evening, Sara made six phone calls. On Thursday, she made four calls. On the weekend, the number of her calls equaled the sum of ten and five times the difference between her Wednesday and Thursday calls.

Sara wrote the following expressions to represent her telephone calls on the weekend.

a. $10 + 5(6 - 4)$ b. $(10 + 5)(6 - 4)$

The grouping of elements in an expression affects the order of operations. This makes a difference in the evaluation of an expression.

A. Evaluate each expression. a = _____ b = _____

B. Which expression correctly represents her situation? _____

Recognize and use order of operations.

Do you know it? Show it:

1 Nicole has a new cell phone plan that gives her 300 minutes less than the square of 80 minutes. Jacob's plan has three times that number of minutes. This expression represents the number of minutes in Jacob's plan.

$$3(80^2 - 300)$$

Name the operation that should be performed first in evaluating the expression.

2 What operation should be performed last in simplifying the expression?

$$x(6 + 2) - 32 + (9 + 10)$$

3 Describe the order of operations that should be used to solve the following problem.

> Connor sent nine text messages to Haley. Haley sent four fewer than twice that many to Jamie. How many messages did they send together?
>
> **9 + (2 • 9 − 4) =**

4 Which grouping yields a solution of 0?

a. $2 \cdot (16 - 5) + 3 \cdot (7 - 4^2)$ c. $(2 \cdot 16) - 5 + 3 \cdot (7 - 4^2)$

b. $(2 \cdot 16) - 5 + (3 \cdot 7) - 4^2$ d. $2 \cdot 16 - (5 + 3) \cdot (7 - 4^2)$

5 Alicia and Monica both simplified the same expression, but they got different results. Examine their work. Which one used the correct order of operations, thus ending up with the correct simplification?

Perform operations with positive and negative numbers.

Do you know it? Show it:

1 While Adam S. Peere was building his hot air balloon business, he was constantly depositing money into, and removing money from, his savings account. Find the sum of the amounts that went through his account.

$1500 + $530 + (–$750) + (–$40) + $1000 + (–$1650) =

2 The difference between –30 and –12 is:
○ –42   ○ 18   ○ –18   ○ 42

3 Circle the letters of any examples that have a solution of –14:

a. $(-4)(7)(-\frac{1}{2}) =$ c. $(-3.5)(-4) =$

b. $\frac{1}{3}(3-6)(14) =$ d. $(-\frac{1}{2})(-\frac{1}{3})(-84) =$

4 Evaluate the expressions. Circle the one with the greatest value.

A. $\frac{(-10+45)}{6-13}$ B. $(83-7) \div (-4)$ C. $\frac{144}{-8}$ D. $(-10^2) \div (-25)$

---

5 A hot air balloon rises 100 feet above the ground. Then it rises another 120 feet and sinks 36 feet. Later it rises 188 feet, followed by two losses of 30 feet. Shortly after that, the balloon rises three intervals, each of 60 feet. Now it is floating along steadily at an even altitude.

A. Which equation represents the current height of the balloon?

a. $100 + 120 - (-36) + 188 + (-2)(-30) + 180$

b. $100 + (-36) + 188 + 2(-30) + 3(60)$

c. $100 + 120 + 188 + 60 - 36 - 30 - 30$

d. $100 + 120 + (-36) + 188 + 2(-30) + 3(60)$

B. What is the height (above the ground) of the hot air balloon now?
○ 492   ○ 558   ○ 564   ○ 372

Perform operations with positive and negative numbers.

Do you know it? Show it:

1 The following amounts show altitude changes in the course of Mr. Imus B. Hire's hot air balloon flight. Find the sum of these changes.

+280 ft   –150 ft   +290 ft   –30 ft
–210 ft   –105 ft   –350 ft   +275 ft

2 If x is a positive integer, which of these has a negative value?

○ $x^3 - x$ ○ $x - (-x)$ ○ $3x - x$ ○ $-x - x$ ○ $-x(x)$

3 Which expression below has the least value?

a. $(-4)^6 (0) =$ c. $-6(4 + 2) =$

b. $(-2)(-3)(-4) =$ d. $(-3 \cdot 2)(-2 \cdot 6) =$

4 Which examples yield a solution of $(-\frac{1}{2})$?

A. $\frac{3.8 - 12.4}{4.2}$ B. $(-2^3) \div 4^2$ C. $\frac{98}{196}$ D. $-4^2 \div (2^3)$

5 Selena soars in a hot air balloon over the Caribbean Sea off the coast of Mexico. Her friend Lucas is scuba diving in the clear water below her. Selena rises to 350 feet above the surface as Lucas descends to a depth of 45 feet below the surface.

Write a subtraction equation using positive and negative integers. Use it to find the difference (d) in feet between the two friends.

Write your equation here.

6a Identify elements of mathematical expressions.

Do you know it? Show it:

1. The expression shows the number of breakfast pastries bought by the McBiscuit family last week.

$$3m + 2(b + s) + 5d$$

a. How many variables are in the expression?

b. Which variable has the greatest coefficient?

The Fluffy Muffin Menu
Muffins (m)   2 for $3.00
Bagels (b) $1.30
Scones (s) $1.75
Doughnuts (d) 5 for $1.00

2. How many like terms are found in the expression below?

$$6n - n^2 + 4pn - (n + p)$$

3. Give one of these labels to each expression:

m *for monomial*   **b** *for binomial*   **p** *for polynomial other than binomial*

a. ___ $\frac{1}{4}z$

b. ___ $x^2 + 8 + x$

c. ___ $2p - q - q^3$

d. ___ $3ab + b$

e. ___ $-5xy$

f. ___ $cd - c$

4. Which examples are not equations?

a. $5cd + d^2 - 2(c + d) = 29$

b. $c^2d - 2(cd) + 3d^2$

c. $6d + c \geq d^3 - 2$

d. $12d > c + c^2$

5. One of the expressions below is a polynomial that can be used to represent the number of pastries in the box. Which is it?

___ $2(d + m) + 4b + c$

___ $2(2b + m + d)$

___ $c + dm + 4b$

___ $2(c + d + m) - c + 4b$

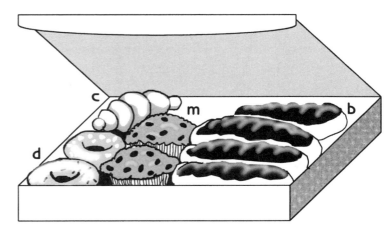

Identify elements of mathematical expressions.

Do you know it? Show it:

1. Adam bought a bag of bagels to share with his soccer team. The expression represents the contents of his bag. (b = blueberry; g = garlic; c = cinnamon; w = wheat; s = sourdough; and p = pumpernickel)

$$4p + 9bw + 5p + 6(pc + g)$$

a. How many variables are in the expression?

b. Which variable has the greatest coefficient?

2. How many *like terms* are found in the expression below?

$xy - 3y^3 + 2y - w + 7y$

3. Which expression is not binomial?

○ $5wz + z$ ○ $ab^2 - b^2 + a + b$ ○ $4xyz + yz$ ○ $\frac{3}{4}g + gh$

4. Label each example: *ex* for *expression*   *in* for *inequality*   *eq* for *equation*

a. ___ $-8p + q \geq p^2 - 4$

b. ___ $x^2yz^2 - 2(xy) + 3z^2$

c. ___ $ab + c^2 - 2(a + b) = 5$

d. ___ $-10n > p + n^2$

---

5. Use the variables on the bagels to create expressions according to the directions. Add other elements to the expression as needed.

a. Write a polynomial expression that includes a coefficient of –6.
_____

b. Write a binomial expression that includes two exponents.
_____

c. Write a polynomial expression with two or more like terms.
_____

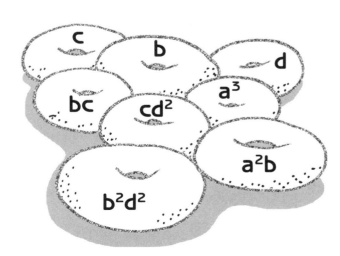

Read and write expressions.

Do you know it? Show it:

1. Max downloaded a number of tunes to his new telephone. Amy purchased a number of tunes that was three times the sum of two and the number that Max added to his phone. Circle the expression that matches the amount of Amy's purchase.

$3m \cdot 3$ $3(2m)$ $3m^2$ $3(m + 2)$

$2(m + 3)$ $3m + 2$ $3m \cdot 2$ $2 + 3m$

2. Which words name this expression? $\frac{2(n-6)}{4}$

     a. one-fourth twice a number subtracted from six

     b. twice the difference between a number and six, divided by four

     c. four divided by two times the difference between a number and six

3. Use numbers and symbols to write the expression.

the product of a number (x) and the sum of that number and seven

4. Write the words to match this expression: **(4a + 2) − b**

---

5. Max spent an amount of money (m) on CDs and downloaded musical tunes. His friend Nate spent an amount that was $18 more than the square of Max's amount. Their friend Brad spent one-half the total amount that Nate and Max spent.

Write an expression that represents the amount Brad spent.

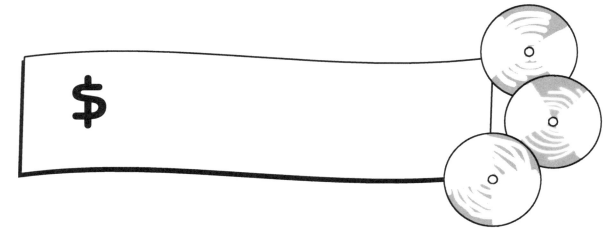

Read and write expressions.

Do you know it? Show it:

1. Haley had 868 tunes on her iPod. She removed a number (n), then reloaded one-third the number she had removed. Circle the expression that represents this situation.

$n + 868$ $\qquad$ $868 - n + \frac{1}{3}n$ $\qquad$ $\frac{868-n}{3}$ $\qquad$ $\frac{1}{3}(868-n)$

2. Which words name this expression? $(6 + x^2) - (y + 3)$

a. the sum of six and a number squared less the sum of another number and three
b. the sum of six and a number squared less the sum of that number and three
c. the difference between a number plus three and six times the square of a number

3. Use numbers and symbols to write the expression.

the product of the cube of a number(b) and the square of another number(d)

4. Write the words to match this expression: $\frac{9(x - y^2)}{2}$

5. Last month Shira spent all of her allowance (a) downloading tunes. This month she spent $7 less than one-third the square of that amount on music. Which expressions could represent the total amount that she spent in the two months?

a. $a + (\frac{1}{3})(\frac{1}{3}a^2 - 7)$

b. $a + \frac{a^2}{3} - 7$

c. $\frac{a + a^2 - 7}{3}$

d. $3a^2 - 7 \div 3$

Simplify and evaluate expressions.

Do you know it? Show it:

1. When Kelly visited the new aquarium, she counted many tiger sharks. Coincidentally, the number of tiger sharks was equal to the sum of the number of other sharks: goblin sharks (g), sawfish (s), mako sharks (m), and horn sharks (h).) She wrote this expression to show that total. Simplify the expression by combining like terms.

$2g^2 - 2m + 5g - 4h - s + 12s + 9h - 5g + 2h^2 + 16m - g^2$

2. Simplify the expressions using properties of operations.

a. Distributive Property: $-4(b - 15 + 3) + b(b - 4)$

b. Additive Identity Property: $24d + 0$

c. Reciprocal Property $(-\frac{1}{4} p)(-4p)$

3. Which expressions are correctly simplified?

○ $3xy + 9x^2 - xy = 2xy + 9x^2$ ○ $-4b(b - 2) = -4b - 8b$

○ $\frac{28n^2}{4n^2} = 7$ ○ $56rs^2 - 7r = 8s$

4. Evaluate the expressions to learn some shark facts.

a. A Mako shark can swim this fast (mph): $\sqrt{400} + \frac{1}{4}(32 \cdot 5)$

b. A whale shark has about this many teeth: $100^2 + (-5^5) - 25(75 + 40)$

c. Of the more than 350 kinds of sharks, this many have been known to attack humans: $(0.001)(30^3)$

5. In each example, evaluate the two expressions.
Place an X in the correct column to describe the comparison of the values.
(Check N if there is not enough information to decide.)

	NOTES	A	B	A > B	B > A	A = B	N
1		$-5\sqrt{169}$	$-29^2 + 2^4$				
2	x is a positive integer	x^2	$-x^2$				
3	n is an integer	$(\frac{1}{2}n)^2$	$0 - n$				
4		$\sqrt[5]{-32}$	$\sqrt[4]{81}$				

Simplify and evaluate expressions.

Do you know it? Show it:

1 The Portuguese shark dives to a greater depth than any other shark. The expression represents this depth. Combine like terms to simplify the expression.

$$\frac{120s^2 - 7s^3 + 15s - s - 2(7s + 6) + 12 + 7s^3}{4s}$$

2 Simplify the expressions using properties of operations.

    a. Reciprocal Property $(-\frac{2}{8})(-4)$

    b. Distributive Property: $6(8 + y - y^2) + y(y + 2)$

    c. Multiplicative Identity Property: $(1)(-5ab^3)$

3 Evaluate the expressions to learn some shark facts.

    a. length of a pygmy ribbontail catshark (inches) $24 - \sqrt{400} + \sqrt{9}$

    b. strength of the dusky shark (pounds of force) $2(4^3) + \sqrt{16}$

    c. migration distance of the blue shark (miles) $40^2 - 3(24 + 6^2) + 4(\sqrt{1600} + 30)$

    d. Find the fact in question #1 (distance in feet). *Let s = 300.*

4 Which expression is correctly simplified?

    ○ $5cd - 3d^2 - (-cd) = 4cd - 3d^2$ ○ $w(12 + w - 2) = w^2 + 10w$

    ○ $\frac{40a^3}{8a} = 5a$ ○ $\frac{9a^2b}{81ab} = \frac{1}{9}$

---

5 Evaluate the following expressions. Let r = 4, s = –5, t = 10, v = –10, and w = 0. Then number the fish in order from least to greatest value.

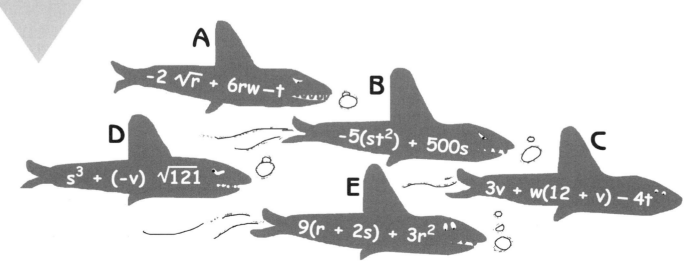

A: $-2\sqrt{r} + 6rw - t$
B: $-5(st^2) + 500s$
C: $3v + w(12 + v) - 4t$
D: $s^3 + (-v)\sqrt{121}$
E: $9(r + 2s) + 3r^2$

Evaluate expressions with roots, radicals, and exponents.

Do you know it? Show it:

1 Sirius A, Barnard's star, and Proxima Centauri are three of the stars (other than the Sun) that are closest to Earth.

Evaluate the expressions to find the distances from Earth in light years.

Sirius A	$72 - 2^6 - \sqrt{81} + 9.6$	_____
Barnard's star	$(\sqrt[4]{16})(\sqrt[3]{27})$	_____
Proxima Centauri	$\sqrt{10{,}000} - 5.8 - \sqrt{8100}$	_____

2 Which group of expressions is in order from least to greatest value?

a. $4^2, 2^5, 5^3, 3^4$ b. $4^2, 2^5, 3^4, 5^3$ c. $3^4, 2^5, 4^2, 5^3$

3 A unit of solar mass (M) is equal to 1.9891 x 1030 kg.

In standard form, this number is _____

4 Express $\frac{1}{9}$ using negative exponents.

○ 3^{-2} ○ 9^{-2} ○ $\frac{1}{9^{-3}}$ ○ (-3^2)

5 For each example, circle the value(s) matching the expression on the star.

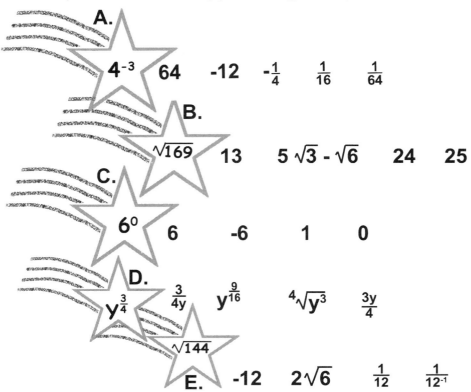

A. 4^{-3} — 64, -12, $-\frac{1}{4}$, $\frac{1}{16}$, $\frac{1}{64}$

B. $\sqrt{169}$ — 13, $5\sqrt{3} - \sqrt{6}$, 24, 25

C. 6^0 — 6, -6, 1, 0

D. $y^{\frac{3}{4}}$ — $\frac{3}{4y}$, $y^{\frac{9}{16}}$, $\sqrt[4]{y^3}$, $\frac{3y}{4}$

E. $\sqrt{144}$ — -12, $2\sqrt{6}$, $\frac{1}{12}$, $\frac{1}{12^{-1}}$

Evaluate expressions with roots, radicals, and exponents.

Do you know it? Show it:

1 Express these space measurements in scientific notation.

    a. distance from Earth to Sun: 93,000,000 mi _____

    b. width of the Sun: 1,400,000 km _____

    c. temperature of Sun at surface: 5800 degrees _____

    d. approximate age of Sun: 4,500,000,000 years _____

2 Circle the group of expressions that is in order from least to greatest value.

    $2^9, 4^5, 5^4, 6^3$ $4^5, 5^4, 2^9, 6^3$ $6^3, 2^9, 5^4, 4^5$

3 Which expressions have a value of $\frac{1}{25}$?

    ○ $\sqrt{\frac{1}{625}}$ ○ 5^{-2} ○ 25^{-1} ○ $(\frac{1}{5})^{-2}$ ○ 5^{-3} ○ $5\sqrt{-3}$

4 Evaluate the expressions.

    a. $\sqrt{(9)(25)}$ c. $\sqrt[7]{128}$ e. $\sqrt{\frac{49}{16}}$

    b. $\sqrt[3]{216}$ d. $\sqrt[3]{-64}$ f. $\frac{2}{\sqrt{25}}$

---

5   A. Circle the correct simplifications.   B. Circle the correct evaluations.

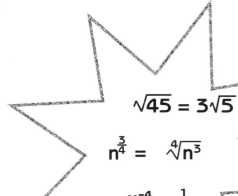

$\sqrt{45} = 3\sqrt{5}$

$n^{\frac{3}{4}} = \sqrt[4]{n^3}$

$x^{-4} = \frac{1}{x^4}$

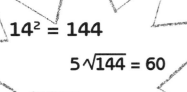

$14^2 = 144$

$5\sqrt{144} = 60$

$\sqrt[4]{256} = 16$

$8^0 = 1$

Perform operations with roots, radicals, and exponents.

Do you know it? Show it:

1 Italy's Mt. Etna is not one of the world's tallest mountains, but it has the longest records of volcanism. It erupts almost continuously. Evaluate the expression to find the height of this mountain (in meters).

$$(5^2)(5^3) + 15^2$$

2 Circle the expressions that have been evaluated correctly.

a. $(4x^3)(6x^4) = 24x^7$ c. $24n^{-6} \div 12n^2 = 2n^{-8}$ e. $(p^6)(p^4) = p^{10}$

b. $21b^9 \div 7b^3 = 3b^6$ d. $(\frac{3}{4})^2 \cdot (\frac{1}{2})^{-2} = (\frac{3}{8})^4$ f. $12^{12} \div 2^2 = 6^6$

3 Write the expressions in order of their values from least to greatest.

a. $(2^2)^4$ b. $(3^3)^2$ c. $[(\frac{3}{4})^2]^2$ d. $(10^0)^6$

4 What is the sum of **4 x 10⁵** and **6 x 10⁴**?

○ 10 x 10²⁰   ○ 4.6 x 10⁴   ○ 4.6 x 10⁵
○ 24 x 10⁹   ○ 24 x 10²⁰   ○ 6.4 x 10⁵

5 Evaluate the expressions to find some of the recent years that Etna has erupted.

A. $(10^9 \div 10^6) + 30^2 + 9^2 + 21$

B. $(2^3)(2^6)(\sqrt[3]{64}) - \sqrt{1600} - 9^0$

C. $(3^3 \cdot 3^2) + (40^8 \div 40^6) + 12^2 - 4^2$

D. $10^2(9+6) + (4^2 \cdot 4^2) + (15^8 \div 15^6) + 3\sqrt{25}$

Perform operations with roots, radicals, and exponents.

Do you know it? Show it:

1. Kilauea, a volcano in Hawaii, is one of the most active in the world. As of 2008, it has been active a number of years, represented by the expression below.

What year did the eruptions begin? _____

$$(\sqrt{169})(\sqrt[3]{64}) - (7^9 \div 7^7) + (2^2)^2 + 2\sqrt{9}$$

2. Circle the expressions that have been evaluated correctly.

a. $(9y^3)(4y^6) = 13y^{18}$ c. $25x^{-5} \div 5x^2 = 5x^{-7}$ e. $(n^3)(n^7) = n^{21}$

b. $22c^{12} \div 2c^7 = 11c^5$ d. $(\frac{1}{4})^3 \cdot (\frac{1}{2})^{-4} = (\frac{1}{18})^{-12}$ f. $6^{-2} \div 3^2 = \frac{1}{16}$

3. Assume that x = 5. Write the expressions in order of their values from least to greatest

a. $(2x^5)^3$ b. $(x^4)^2$ c. $(\frac{1}{2}x^2)^6$ d. $(x^3)^2$ e. $(x^0)^9$

4. What is the sum of **7 x 10⁴** and **3 x 10⁵**?

○ 21×10^{20} ○ 7.3×10^4 ○ 3.7×10^{-1}

○ 3.7×10^5 ○ 21×10^9 ○ 3.7×10^4

5. Solve the problems to find the facts for a – d.

a. _____ ft
b. _____ m
c. _____ yrs
d. _____

Kilauea Facts

Location: Big Island of Hawaii

Meaning of Name: "spewing"

a. Elevation (ft): $(\sqrt{160,000})(\sqrt{100}) + 2(3^4) + 28$
b. Depth of summit caldera (ft): $2(9^2) + \sqrt[4]{81}$
c. Oldest dated rocks: $(10^3 \cdot 5^2) - 80(5^2)$
d. Number of recorded eruptions: $\frac{2^9}{2^3} - \sqrt[3]{27}$

Recognize and use factors and multiples.

Do you know it? Show it:

1 Some critters are invading Patrick's basement. He and his sister count the legs and get an amazing total of 576.
  a. If these are insects (6 legs), how many are there?
  b. If these critters are spiders (8 legs), how many are there?
  c. If these are mice (4 legs), how many are there?

2 What factors are common to 420, 630, 42, and 210?

3 Which is the prime factorization of 84?
  a. 12 • 7   c. 2 • 3 • 3 • 7   e. 4 • 21
  b. 2 • 2 • 3 • 7   d. 7 • 3 • 4   f. 2 • 6 • 7

4 What is the numerical difference between the least common multiple and the greatest common factor of the numbers 8, 12, 20, 16?
  ○ 12   ○ 18   ○ 120   ○ 156   ○ 238   ○ 638   ○ 472

5 Each fly can get caught only in a part of the web that has a number divisible by that fly's number, with no remainder. Tell which numbers in the web are dangerous for each fly.

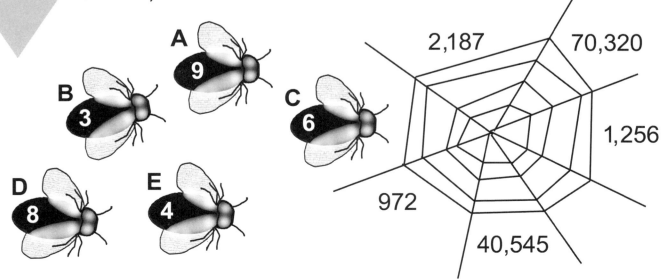

Recognize and use factors and multiples.

Do you know it? Show it:

1 There are about 2,007 different species of scorpions. About 897 different species of tarantulas have been identified. A survey at Jefferson Middle School found that 615 students had arachnophobia.

    a. What is the greatest common factor of these numbers? _____

    b. How many of these numbers are divisible by 9? _____

2 Here's the prime factorization: **2 • 3² • 5 • 7**. What's the number?

    210   420   23   214   630   580

3 What factors are common to 240, 120, and 360? _____

4 What is the numerical difference between the least common multiple and the greatest common factor of the numbers 15, 6, 3, 18?

    ○ 87   ○ 39   ○ 159   ○ 537   ○ 270   ○ 1,617

---

5 The population of ants in an anthill outside Jennifer's house is a number with these characteristics:

It is the smallest 4-digit number that is divisible by 2, 4, 5, 8, 9, and 10.

The greatest common factor that the number shares with 99 is 9.

The sum of the digits is 9.

What is the number?

Perform operations with fractions and decimals.

Do you know it? Show it:

1 A package of Hershey's kisses identifies the serving size as nine kisses. One serving of original kisses contains 230 calories. How many calories are found in one kiss?

(Write a problem that uses a fraction as a factor and yields a fractional answer.)

_____

2 Solve: (3.5 − 1.07) (1.5) =

3 Compare the solutions to the problems below.
Circle: A > B   or   B > A   or   A = B

   A. 99.09 + 1.999   B. 463.3 ÷ 4.1

4 Which problems have a solution of $\frac{2}{3}$?

   a. $\frac{1}{6} + \frac{4}{3} - \frac{5}{4} + \frac{5}{12} =$ c. $\frac{1}{2} \div \frac{3}{4} =$ e. $1\frac{5}{6} \div \frac{23}{4} =$

   b. $\frac{10}{21} \cdot 1\frac{2}{5} =$ d. $\frac{3}{4} \div \frac{8}{9} =$ f. $\frac{7}{12} \cdot \frac{8}{7} =$

---

5 It takes 95 chocolate kisses to equal a pound of chocolate.
Emma puts 3.5 pounds of kisses into a bag.
Evan comes along and takes out 1.05 pounds.
Emma adds four groups of 9.75 pounds.
Evan removes 11.45 pounds.

   a. How many pounds are left in the bag? _____

   b. How many kisses is this? _____

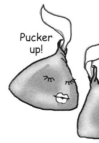

Perform operations with fractions and decimals.

Do you know it? Show it:

1. A chocolate kiss has a diameter (at the bottom) of .875 inch. It is wrapped in shiny foil that is $2\frac{1}{4}$ inches square. (Use 3.14 as the value of π.)

   a. When the kiss is set on a table, how much area will it cover? _____

   b. If this foil is spread out flat, how much area will it cover? _____

2. Solve: $(8.9 - 6.38)(.001) =$

3. Compare the solutions to the problems below.
Circle: A > B   or   B > A   or   A = B

   A. $\frac{6}{16} + \frac{3}{4} + 5\frac{1}{4}$ 　　　　　 B. $10\frac{3}{4} \div 2\frac{1}{2}$

4. Write the answers in simplest form.

   a. $\frac{3ab}{b} \div \frac{4b}{2c} =$ 　　　 b. $2\frac{1}{2} \cdot 5\frac{3}{4} =$ 　　　 c. $\frac{5}{6} - \frac{8}{12} + \frac{1}{3} =$

5. The little strip of paper that helps to unwrap a chocolate kiss is about $2\frac{3}{4}$ inches long. Which of the strips below will yield a solution equivalent to this number?

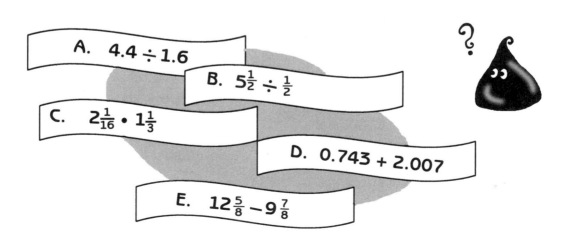

A. $4.4 \div 1.6$

B. $5\frac{1}{2} \div \frac{1}{2}$

C. $2\frac{1}{16} \cdot 1\frac{1}{3}$

D. $0.743 + 2.007$

E. $12\frac{5}{8} - 9\frac{7}{8}$

Solve problems with percent.

Do you know it? Show it:

1 China is the world's largest exporter of fireworks, producing about 45 million cases a year (almost 1 million tons). Six million of these cases are sold to businesses in the United States. This is what percent of China's total annual production? (Round to the nearest tenth.)

2 Forty percent of U.S. states permit the sale of most types of consumer fireworks to the general public. How many states permit these sales?

3 Solve:

a. 68 is what % of 80? _____   c. 250 is 40% of what number? _____

b. What is 136% of 25? _____   d. 17 is what % of 68? _____

4 Shannon bought a case of firecrackers on sale at a 25% discount. She paid $21.00.
What was the original price? _____

5 Read the fireworks situations. Answer the questions with the letter of the matching answer. (Use N for *none of these*.)
Which example demonstrates a:

a. 29.17% increase? _____   d. 133% increase? _____

b. 40% increase? _____   e. 32% decrease? _____

c. 42% decrease? _____   f. 500% decrease? _____

A. Ina and Kayla intended to buy 85 each of five different kinds of sparklers. Due to a good sale, they bought a total of 595 sparklers instead.

B. Last year, there were 24 reported cases of fireworks injuries in the city. This year, 31 injuries were reported.

C. On Jason's first trip to Wonder World Amusement Park, the fireworks display lasted 75 minutes. On his next visit, the display lasted 51 minutes.

D. Cost of a local Chinese New Year celebration included a $349,500 fireworks expense. The previous year's fireworks cost $150,000.

Solve problems with percent.

Do you know it? Show it:

1 In the United States, five states ban the sale and use of all consumer fireworks. Another four states permit the sale of wood stick sparklers only. All other states allow sale of fireworks according to rules more lenient than these. What percent of the states do the wider rules represent?

2 What is $\frac{13}{3}$ expressed as a percent? (Shade the circle.)

○ 4.33% ○ .214% ○ 1.4% ○ 43.3%

○ 433.3% ○ 2.14% ○ 214% ○ .433%

3 The fireworks stand at the corner of North Countrywide Lane pays $45 for a carton of 100 bottle rockets. The selling price of each bottle rocket is $1.35. What is the percent of increase in the sale price over their purchase price?

4 Solve:

a. 26 is what % of 40? _____   c. 140 is 28% of what number? _____

b. What is 225% of 72? _____   d. 87 is what % of 75? _____

5 A fireworks factory packed an order that included the items shown in the illustration. Use the information to answer the questions. Round percents to the nearest tenth.

Box #1
45 sparklers
20 sky rockets
40 flares
25 cherry bombs
10 Roman candles

Box #2
12 Roman candles
100 firecrackers
88 flares
10 cherry bombs

a. What item made up 10% of the entire order?
_____

b. What percent of Box #1 consisted of flares?
_____

c. What percent of Box #2 consisted of Roman candles?
_____

d. What item made up 32.1% of Box #1?
_____

I've Got It!—Pre-Algebra Skills
Copyright ©2008 by Incentive Publications, Inc., Nashville, TN.

Factor expressions.

Do you know it? Show it:

1. On 12 consecutive days, Sheriff Bea Kurious received reports of Bigfoot sightings. On each of these days, she heard from the same number of groups of campers. The number in each group was the cube of a number she didn't reveal (y). All of these group members claimed to have seen Bigfoot. Sheriff Kurious wrote this expression to represent the number of sightings.

$$12ny^3$$

Which of the following are prime factors of this expression?

    -12 2 3 y $3n$ 4 5 6 n ny y^2

2. What is the greatest common factor of $18ab^2$, $54a^4$, and $60ab^3$?

3. Which of the following could not be a factor of $-8p^2qr$?

○ $4q$ ○ pr ○ q ○ p^2 ○ r^2 ○ -2

4. Show two possible factorizations for **$-24x^4$**.

_____   _____

5. Which expressions are correctly factored?

A $-12n^6$ $(6n^2)(-2n^4)$

B $4x^2y^5z$ $(xy^4z)(4xy)$

C $15a^3b^2c$ $(-5a^2b^2)(-3ac)$

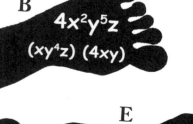

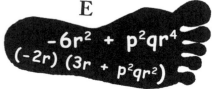

Factor expressions and equations.

Do you know it? Show it:

1. Max and Maxine were shocked and thrilled to stumble upon a huge footprint in the forest near the Pacific coast. They measured the footprint with the only tools they had: pebbles (p), shells (s), and mini chocolate bars (c). They wrote this expression to describe the length of the footprint:

$$56s + 2c^2 + 4pc$$

Which of the following are prime factors of this expression?

    13   5   2   s   4   7   8   c   11   p c^2

2. What is the greatest common factor of $32xy^3$, $12xy^2$, and $80x^3y$?

3. Which of the following could *not* be factors of $-21x^4y^2z$?

  ○ $7x^2$ ○ $9y^2$ ○ q   ○ $-3yz$ ○ z^2 ○ xyz

4. Show two possible factorizations for $72a^2b^5$.

_____   _____

5. Which expressions are correctly factored?

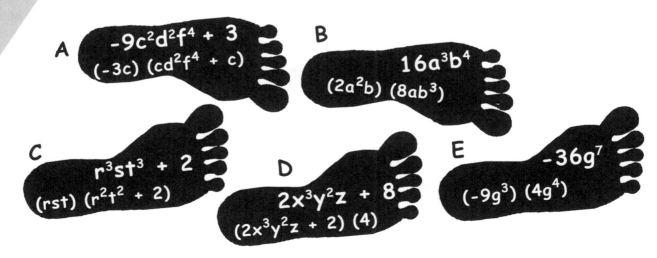

A. $-9c^2d^2f^4 + 3$ $(-3c)(cd^2f^4 + c)$

B. $16a^3b^4$ $(2a^2b)(8ab^3)$

C. $r^3st^3 + 2$ $(rst)(r^2t^2 + 2)$

D. $2x^3y^2z + 8$ $(2x^3y^2z + 2)(4)$

E. $-36g^7$ $(-9g^3)(4g^4)$

Translate problems into equations.

Do you know it? Show it:

1. The 2007 pirate movie *Pirates of the Caribbean: At World's End* took in a large sum of money in its first three days. However, this amount was $21 million less than the amount taken in by the previous POC movie, *Dead Man's Chest*. The total gross income for the two movies in their first three days was $251 million. Which equation is the best one for finding the amount (in millions) taken in by *At World's End*?

   a. $21x = 251$ b. $251 = 2x + 21$ c. $21 + x = 251$ d. $x + x - 21 = 251$

2. A pirate ship, *The Stingray*, traveled a total of 88 miles in one week. She traveled 18 miles farther on Friday than on Thursday. On all the other days of the week, the ship covered half the miles traveled on Thursday.

Will the equation below find the miles traveled on Thursday?
$$d + (d + 18) + (5 \cdot \tfrac{1}{2}d) = 88$$

3. Which equation solves the problem?

Find n if 34 is half the sum of the cube of n and its square root.

   a. $\tfrac{1}{2}n^3 + \sqrt{n} = 34$ b. $\dfrac{(n^3 + \sqrt{n})}{2} = 34$ c. $2(2n^2 + \sqrt{n}) = 34$

4. Pirate ship A sets sail heading west. Ship B, 1,000 miles away, sets sail 2 hours later heading east. They both travel at 25 miles an hour on the same course. If there are no variations in weather or other conditions, how long will it take for the ships to meet?

Write an equation to solve the problem.

5. Pirate Pete buried a cache of gold doubloons. His friend, Gunpowder Gracie, buried 200 less than twice the square of Pete's stash. Their unfriendly foe, Captain Catsup, hid away half the number of doubloons that Gracie buried. Together, the three pirates buried 4,540 coins.

How many coins did Pete bury?

   a. $4{,}540 - x - 2x = 200 + 2x^2$
   b. $x + 2x^2 + 200 + \tfrac{1}{2}x^2 = 4{,}540$
   c. $x + (2x^2 - 200) + \tfrac{1}{2}(2x^2 - 200) = 4{,}540$

Which equation will find the number of coins Pete buried?

Translate problems into equations.

Do you know it? Show it:

1. A pirate ship, *The Silver Dagger*, traveled 380 miles over ten days to reach a remote island where the pirates intended to bury treasure. The ship covered 65 miles on each of the first three days. On the other seven days, the ship traveled an equal number of miles each day. Which equation is the best one for finding the number of miles traveled on the tenth day?

   a. $3(65 + 7x) = 380$ b. $380 - 3(65 + 7) = x$ c. $(3 \cdot 65) + 7x = 380$

2. Treasure chest A holds 840 coins more than half the amount in chest B. Together, the chests hold 2,040 coins. Write an equation that will find the number of coins in chest A.

3. Which equation solves the problem?

Find y if its square is 28 less than the cube of eight.

   a. $8^3 - \sqrt{y} = 28$ b. $8^3 - 28 = y^2$ c. $8(y^2)(3) = 512$

4. Pirate Annie McLoud heads west from the beach, looking for a treasure that is buried on the island 48 miles due west. She starts at 8 A.M. and walks at a steady pace. (It's a slow pace, due to an ankle that was damaged by a crocodile bite.) She arrives at the treasure site at midnight. Will this equation find her rate of travel?

$$12x - 8x = 48$$

5. The number of reported pirate attacks in 2007 was 24 greater than the number reported in 2006. Together, the number of attacks totaled 502. It is estimated that only 10%–50% of pirate attacks are actually reported.

A. Which equation (at right) will find the attacks reported in 2006?

B. Which equation (at right) will find the attacks reported in 2007?

C. If only 10% of the attacks were reported in 2007, how many attacks actually occurred in that year?

a. $2n + 24 = 502$
b. $n + 24 = 502$
c. $\frac{1}{2}(n + 24) = 502$
d. $502 = 2n - 24$

Solve equations using inverse operations.

Do you know it? Show it:

1. Use the property of inverse operations to find the solution.

A rat ate through two pieces of cheese. The first piece took 12 minutes to eat. It took him 27 minutes to eat both pieces. How long did the second piece take?

$$27 - t = 12 \qquad t = \underline{\qquad}$$

2. What is the value of x in the equation?   **−12 + x = 4**

○ 8   ○ −16   ○ 20   ○ 16   ○ −8

3. Which equations have a solution of (−10)?

a. $\frac{40}{x} = (-4)$ b. $(-100) = \frac{-x}{-5}$ c. $2100 \div x = (-210)$ d. $\frac{x}{8} = (-2)$

4. Write an equation to represent the problem. Find the solution.

One rat weighs 9 ounces. This is 12 times the weight of a second rat. What is the weight of the second rat (w)?

_____   w = _____

---

5. Much to the shock of diners, a group of fine city restaurants began having problems with rats. An equation represents the number found in each restaurant. Solve each equation for the number of rats (r). Use the chart below to compare the numbers. For each pair, put an X in one of the columns: A > B, B > A, or A = B.

Number of Rats Found in City Restaurants in One Week

	Restaurant A	Restaurant B	A>B	B>A	A = B
1	Chez Pierre $9r = 135$	Le Bistro $r - 23 = 40$			
2	Antonio's $\frac{88}{r} = 4$	La Scala $5r + (-33) = 47$			
3	Ocar D Cafe $r \div 48 = .5$	Alexandria $480 = 5r$			

Solve equations using inverse operations.

16b

Do you know it? Show it:

1 Use the property of inverse operations to find the solution.

A group of 20 rats ate all but a few inches of a giant sausage. To start, the sausage was 30 inches long. When the rats gave up, 4 inches remained. How much did the rats eat?

$$30 - s = 4 \qquad s = _____$$

2 What is the value of x in the equation? $x + (-6) = -5$

○ 1 ○ -11 ○ -1 ○ 11 ○ -2

3 Which equations have a solution of (–5)?

a. $-400 \div x = (8)$ b. $\frac{60}{x} = (-12)$ c. $(-1) = \frac{-x}{5}$ d. $\frac{x}{(-.5)} = (-10)$

4 Write an equation to represent the problem. Find the solution.

A Norway rat can be as long as 50 centimeters (including the tail). A group of the largest rats line up nose to tail tip. The line is 1,500 cm long. How many rats (r) are in the line?

_____ **r =** _____

5 Two hundred rats are being taught to find their way through a complicated maze. Group A completes the task in a number of minutes. Group B completes the task in 2 minutes more than three times the length of time taken by group A. Group C completes the task in one-half the time of Group A. The sum of the time taken by all three groups is 56 minutes. How much time has Group A taken to learn the maze?

a. $2t + \frac{1}{2}(3t + 2) = 56$
b. $56 - t - 2t - 3t + 2 = t$
c. $4\frac{1}{2}t + 2 = 56$
d. $t + 2t + 3(t + 2) = 56$
e. $t = 56 - 3\frac{1}{2}t - 2$

A. Choose an equation (above) that will solve the problem.
B. Find the solution.

I've Got It!—Pre-Algebra Skills
Copyright ©2008 by Incentive Publications, Inc., Nashville, TN.

Solve equations with one variable and one step.

Do you know it? Show it:

1. A deep-sea diver descends six times deeper than his friend—to a depth of 252 feet. How far (d) did his friend descend?
Write and solve an equation to find the answer.

2. If **−7y = −784**, then y =

○ −5488   ○ 777   ○ 112   ○ 791

○ −112   ○ −791   ○ 5488   ○ −777

3. Find the value of b in the equation. $\frac{-45}{b} = 3$

4. What is the negative value of x in the equation? $x^2 = 196$

---

5. Solve each equation for (f) to find the number of fish photographed by each diver.

Tyler	$20.4 - (-f) = 60.4$	**James**	$\sqrt{f} = 13$
Emily	$f^3 = 8000$	**Charlene**	$f + (-20) = 47$
Gabe	$\frac{126}{f} = 4.5$	**Maria**	$6.2f = 545.6$

Say, "Cheese."

A. The equation $\frac{a}{b} = \frac{1}{2}$ represents the relationship between the numbers of fish photographed by which two divers?

B. The equation **4.4c = d** represents the relationship between the numbers of fish photographed by which two divers?

Solve equations with one variable and one step.

Do you know it? Show it:

1 Matt, a seasoned diver, has explored 68 different shipwrecks in the world. This is one-fifth the number of wrecks explored by his friend Hannah. How many shipwrecks has she explored?

Write and solve an equation to find the answer.

2 If **−12a = 192**, then **a** =

○ −204   ○ 180   ○ 204   ○ −180
○ 26   ○ 16   ○ −16   ○ −2304

3 Find the value of *n* in the equation. $\frac{78}{n} = (-13)$

4 What is the negative value of x in the equation?   **$x^2 = 20.25$**

5 An afternoon expedition takes divers to explore several shipwrecks. The divers on this trip have a wide range of experience in terms of numbers of dives. Find the correct solution for each equation to complete each diver's record.

Divers' Experience

Diver	Number of Dives
Benjamin B.	$\frac{3}{4}x = 33$
Dionne R.	$\sqrt{x} = 16$
Jasmine C.	$-84 - (-x) = -72$
Maria S.	$12.2x = 36.6$
Anna T.	$\frac{x}{20} = 1\frac{3}{5}$

44 4
99 32 26
1   121 18
12 68 3 256

Solve multi-step equations.

Do you know it? Show it:

1. When Sam learned to surf as an 8-year-old, he was thrilled to ride a wave that seemed big to him. Twelve years later, he has just taken a great ride on a 44-foot wave. This is 10 feet less than twice the cube of his first wave's height. How tall was that first wave?

Choose and solve the equation that will answer the question.

    a. $44 = 2(10 + x^3)$ c. $2x^3 - 10 = 44$

    b. $44 - 10 - x^3 = x$ d. $x(12 - 8) = 44$

2. Solve equations A and B. Then circle one of the statements below.

    A. $5(2d - 4) - 3d = 12d$ B. $18 + 4c(4 - 2) = (-c)$

Which is true of the solutions?   A > B   B > A   A = B

3. What is the value of **p** in the following equation?

$$3(p + 5)(2 + 3) - 30 = 18p + 33$$

4. What are the solutions to the following equation?

$$n^2 - 7n + 12 = 0$$

○ (–3) and (–2)   ○ 6 and 3   ○ 2 and (–6)

○ (–3) and –4   ○ 4 and 3   ○ 6 and 3

5. When surfers talk about "hanging ten" and "hanging five," they are referring to moves on a longboard (9- to 10-ft surfboard). When both feet are on the front of the board, all ten toes are off the edge. When one foot is near the front, only five toes "hang." One morning, a number of surfers are riding longboards. Some are "hanging ten." Eight less than twice as many are "hanging five." There are a total of 200 toes hanging.

A. Choose and solve an equation that will find the number of surfers "hanging ten".

    a. $10(x) + 5(2x - 8) = 200$

    b. $\frac{1}{10}x + \frac{1}{5}x - 8 = 200$

    c. $200 \div (10x + 5x - 8) = x$

B. How many surfers are riding? _____

C. How many are "hanging five"? _____

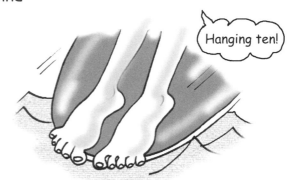

Solve multi-step equations.

Do you know it? Show it:

1. Vanessa waited for a great wave. Several waves passed before she caught the right one for a great ride. Before her second ride, she let eight more than one-third the number of the first ride go by. In all, Vanessa let 40 waves go by as she chose the right waves for these two rides. How many went by before her first ride?

Choose and solve the equation that will answer the question.

a. $(40 + 8) \div 3 = w$ c. $3(40 + 8) = w$ e. $w + \frac{1}{3}w + 8 = 40$

b. $w + \frac{(w + 8)}{3} = 40$ d. $40w - \frac{1}{3}w - 8 = w$ f. $w + \frac{1}{3}w - 8 = 40$

2. Solve equations A and B. Then circle one of the statements below.

A. $-2(p - 3) = 4p$ B. $-3(q + 6) = 3q$

Which is true of the solutions?   A > B   B > A   A = B

3. What is the value of **m** in the following equation?

$$\frac{6(m + 9)}{-3} + (-m) = 0$$

4. A. Which equation below shows a correct solution for $x = 5$? _____
B. Which equation below shows a correct solution for **x = (–5)**? _____

a. $2x(x + 2) - 50 = 70$ c. $2x(x + 2) - 50 = 20$

b. $2x(x + 2) - 50 = -20$ d. $2x(x + 2) - 50 = 30$

---

5. The age of three surfers totals 63. Angela is half Brad's age. Brad is one-third Charlie's age.

A. Write and solve an equation to help find the ages.

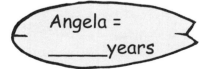 Angela = ____ years

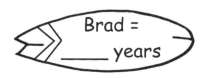 Brad = ____ years

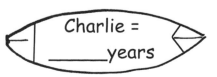 Charlie = ____ years

B. In seven years, Angela will be two-thirds of Brad's age. Write a fraction to show the relationship of Charlie's age to Brad's age in seven years.

Solve equations with rational numbers.

Do you know it? Show it:

1 Six friends share a giant pizza, each eating a slice of equal size. Every slice has an outside crust edge measuring 9.42 inches. What is the diameter of the pizza? Solve the equation to answer the question:

$$\frac{\pi d}{6} = 9.42$$

2 Is the sum of $\frac{2n}{8} + \frac{(n+12)}{4}$ greater than n if n = 9?

3 What is the value of x in the equation $\frac{x}{(5x+3)} = 1$?

    a. $x = -\frac{3}{4}$ b. $x = \frac{4}{3}$ c. $x = 12$ d. $x = \frac{3}{4}$

4 Solve the equations. Describe the relationship of the solutions to one another.

    a. $\frac{2}{3}x = \frac{1}{6}$ c. $p + \frac{1}{8} = \frac{7}{8}$

    b. $9 \div \frac{1}{n} = 4\frac{1}{2}$ d. $\frac{8}{a} - \frac{24}{3} = 0$

5 Four busloads of hockey players stopped at The Pizza Den for a post-tournament meal. The staff had planned ahead and had a large number of pizzas ready. Players from the first bus ate one-sixth of the pizzas. The next busload ate two-sixths of the original number. The third group ate two-fifths of the remaining pizzas. This left $28\frac{4}{5}$ pizzas for the last group.

Write and solve an equation to find information to finish the chart.

a. the original number of pizzas (p)_____

b. number of pizzas eaten by the first group_____

c. number of pizzas eaten by the second group_____

d. number of pizzas eaten by the third group_____

Solve equations with rational numbers.

Do you know it? Show it:

1 A pizza with a 7-inch radius is divided into 12 equal pieces. What is the measure of the outside crust edge of each piece? (Round to the nearest tenth.)
Solve the equation to find the answer:

$$m = \frac{\pi(2 \cdot 7)}{12}$$

2 Is the sum of $\frac{5n + 10}{3} + \frac{-4n - 14}{6}$ greater than n if n = –6?

3 Circle the value of x in the equation $\frac{x}{4x - 5} = \frac{2}{7}$

$x = 1$ $x = \frac{1}{10}$ $x = \frac{2}{5}$ $x = 10$ $x = 2$ $x = \frac{7}{4}$

4 Solve the equations. Describe the relationship of the solutions to one another.

a. $\frac{2}{3} v = -1\frac{1}{3}$

b. $w \div \frac{4}{7} = (-7)$

c. $\frac{9}{20} - y = 6\frac{9}{20}$

d. $\frac{5}{7} z = (-\frac{40}{7})$

5 Chef Louisa is a master pizza-dough tosser. She warms up with a modest toss (t). The second toss is $1\frac{1}{2}$ times the first. The third toss is $2\frac{1}{3}$ times the second. It is 14 feet high.

A. How high is the first toss? _____

B. How high is the second toss? _____

C. If another toss is $1\frac{3}{4}$ times the second toss, how high will it be? _____

20a Solve equations with radicals and exponents.

Do you know it? Show it:

1 An octopus, of course, has eight tentacles. A group of octopi is joined by a second group that is equal in number to $\sqrt{225}$ times the number in the first group. The entire gathering has a total of 512 tentacles. Choose and solve the equation that will find the number of octopi in the first group.

a. $8(x + x\sqrt{225}) = 512$

b. $\dfrac{x + x(\sqrt{225})}{8} = 512$

c. $8x \div 512 = \sqrt{225}$

d. $8(x + \sqrt{225}) = 512$

2 Which equation is not solved correctly?

A. $5x - \sqrt{81} = 101$
   $x = 22$

B. $(n^3)^2 = 64$
   $n = 8$

3 Solve for y: $(\sqrt{y^2})(y^2) = 729$

4 If x is (–5), what is the missing number in the equation below?
$4x^2 + x = \boxed{}$

5

a. A female octopus lays a number of eggs that can be represented by the equation below:

$$n = (2.0 \times 10^5) - (2.0 \times 10^4)$$

What is the number of eggs (in standard notation)? _____

b. An octopus has two rows of suckers on each tentacle. Scientist Dr. Maurine Marine studies a particular octopus and finds 100 suckers in each row. Written in scientific notation, how many suckers will be found on this animal (on all the tentacles?)

_____

Solve equations with radicals and exponents.

Do you know it? Show it:

1. The largest octopus, the Giant Pacific Octopus, can have tentacles of a surprising length. To find this length, solve the equation below. (Length is in feet per tentacle.)

$6 + t + 88 = 127$ $t =$ _____ ft

2. Circle the letter(s) of equation(s) below that are not solved correctly.

A. $a^2\sqrt{121} = 55$
    $a = 5$

B. $2b^3 + 12 = 66$
    $b = 4$

3. Solve for the positive solution to x:

$3x^4 - \sqrt{144} = 36$

4. What is the negative solution to the following equation?

$x^3 + \sqrt{144} = -52$

5.

a. A Giant Pacific Octopus is a weighty animal. The weight of a group of 800 is represented by this equation: $800x = (4.2 \times 10^5) + (6.0 \times 10^4)$ lbs.

What is the weight of one of these octopi? _____ pounds

b. To defend itself, this octopus can expel a large ink cloud. The dimensions of the cloud are represented by this equation: $d^3 = 1.0 \times 10^3$. What are the dimensions of such an ink cloud (in standard notation)? _____ ft Give one set of numbers (height, width, and depth) that would result in this number.

Find rate, time, and distance.

Do you know it? Show it:

1 A train travels 2,100 miles west from Memphis, stopping four times for an hour each stop. The total travel time (including the stops) is 34 hours. Two of the following equations will be helpful in finding the train's rate (in miles per hour). Circle them. Then find the train's average speed. Rate = _____

   a. $2100 = 34r$ c. $\frac{2100}{r} = 34 - 4$ e. $30r = 2100$

   b. $2100r = 34$ d. $34r = 2100$ f. $34 \div r = 2100$

2 Find time (t) if distance (d) = 426 mi and rate (r) = 35.5 mph.

   t = _____

3 Train A travels 80 miles an hour for 18 hours.
Train B travels 85 miles per hour for 16 hours.

a. Which train travels farther? _____

b. What is the difference between their distances? _____

4 The dining car on the *West Ghost Cruiser* serves meals seven days a week. The *Cruiser* makes three round trips a day between two small ghost towns. In a week, the chef prepares 6,300 meals. On average, how many meals are served on each trip?

5 The *ABC Train* travels east at 68 miles per hour. The *XYZ Train* leaves a station 3,220 miles east at exactly the same time, and follows the same route heading west. *XYZ* travels at an average of 72 miles per hour. Both trains depart their stations at 11:59 P.M. Central Standard Time on Friday.

a. When will the trains meet? _____

b. How far will the XYZ Train have traveled when they meet? _____

Find rate, time, and distance.

Do you know it? Show it:

1. A train travels from Oregon to the Mexican border at a rate of 82 mph. The train covers a distance of 1,230 miles, stopping five times for one hour each time. Write and solve an equation that will help find the traveling time.

How long did the trip take (including stopping time)? _____

2. Find rate (r) if distance (d) = 456 mi and time (t) = $9\frac{1}{2}$ hr.

r = _____

3. A train trip lasts 20 hours. The train travels at 75 mph and stops twice, for one hour each time. A car trip lasts 30 hours. The car travels at an average speed of 65 mph and stops five times for one hour each time.

a. Which vehicle travels the greater distance? _____

b. What is the difference between their distances? _____

4. A zoo train carried visitors around the zoo grounds, making 14 trips a day, every day for two weeks. The train was full on every trip. The total number of passengers carried in that two weeks was 5,880. How many passengers could the train hold?

n = _____

5. Dexter boards a train traveling north. His friend Derek boards a train 1,512 miles away traveling south on the same route. They plan to meet at a stop that is 720 miles from the city where Dexter has begin his trip. The trains arrive at this station at the same time after both have traveled for 12 hours.

a. At what rate will Dexter's train have traveled? _____

b. At what rate will Derek's train have traveled?

_____

Solve problems with ratio and proportion.

Do you know it? Show it:

1 Sydney earned money by walking dogs every day during the last two weeks in March. He walked the same number each day, for a total of 126 dogs. At this rate, how many dogs did he walk in three days?

Circle the proportion that will solve the problem. Find the solution. _____

a. $\dfrac{126}{2} = \dfrac{3}{n}$ b. $\dfrac{n}{7} = \dfrac{126}{3}$ c. $\dfrac{126}{14} = \dfrac{n}{3}$ d. $\dfrac{14}{126} = \dfrac{7}{3}$

2 Cross-multiply to solve the proportions.

a. $\dfrac{20}{35} = \dfrac{4}{x}$ x =   b. $\dfrac{\frac{5}{3}}{25} = \dfrac{x}{60}$ x =   c. $\dfrac{x}{12} = \dfrac{100}{20}$ x =

3 Circle any ratios that do NOT form a proportion with $\dfrac{8}{3}$.

$\dfrac{24}{6}$ $\dfrac{88}{33}$ $\dfrac{96}{60}$ $\dfrac{48}{18}$

4 Express each ratio as a fraction in simplest form.

a. number of days in six weeks to those in a leap year

b. $8ab^3 : 20ab^2$

c. $\dfrac{28xy}{98x}$

5 Victor walks four dogs to the park every day.

A map that shows his route has a scale of 3 inches = 2 miles.

Victor walks from his home to pick up Max. This distance is $\frac{1}{2}$ inch on the map.

He and Max walk to fetch Lucy. This distance is $\frac{3}{4}$ inch.

Victor, Max, and Lucy walk to Boe's home. This distance is $1\frac{1}{2}$ inch.

The three dogs and Victor pick up Chachi—another 1 inch.

From Chachi's home, it is $\frac{3}{4}$ inch to the park.

After two hours of playing in the park, Victor retraces his steps.

How far, in real distance, has Victor walked?

Solve problems with ratio and proportion.

Do you know it? Show it:

1 Residents in the Main Street East neighborhood have a total of 12 dogs. The Main Street West neighbors have a total of 54 dogs.

What ratio forms a proportion with the comparison of the East to West neighborhood dogs?

a. $\frac{6}{8}$ b. $\frac{3}{1}$ c. $\frac{2}{9}$ d. $\frac{9}{2}$ e. $\frac{3}{12}$ f. $\frac{12}{3}$ g. $\frac{1}{3}$

2 Cross-multiply to solve the proportions.

a. $\frac{143}{x} = \frac{121}{11}$ x =

b. $\frac{6}{15} = \frac{30}{x}$ x =

c. $\frac{56}{112} = \frac{x}{16}$ x =

3 Which ratio forms a proportion with $\frac{8}{22}$?

○ $\frac{4}{12}$ ○ $\frac{4}{11}$ ○ $\frac{11}{4}$ ○ $\frac{1}{3}$ ○ $\frac{2}{6}$ ○ $\frac{6}{2}$

4 Express each ratio as a fraction in simplest form.

a. 5 months to 15 years

b. $18cd^4f^2 : 63cdf$

c. $\frac{116xyz}{58xy}$

5 In her profession as a dog walker, Nicole needs to buy plenty of dog biscuits.

Last month, she fed 80 biscuits to 16 dogs in one day.

a. At this rate, how many dogs would it take to use 120 biscuits? _____

b. At this rate, on what day will she use the last of a bag of 2,000 biscuits? _____

c. How many biscuits would be needed a day if she fed 28 dogs? _____

Use ratios to show probability.

Do you know it? Show it:

1 Sam has a set of cubes with 1–6 dots on each side (dice). A pair of these are tossed. Write a ratio to show the probability of a result of both cubes showing one dot.

2 The spinner is spun once.
What is the probability that the result will NOT be a prime number?

3 Charlene is handed a pile of unlabeled envelopes. Each one contains a bill.
Three envelopes hold a $50 bill; one holds a $100 bill; two hold $20s; six hold $5s and two hold $10s. She is allowed to choose one envelope.
What are the odds in favor of her choosing an envelope with an amount greater than $10?

4 Taylor takes three pairs of jeans, five shirts, and two jackets on a trip. How many different outfits can he wear that includes one of each category?

○ 10   ○ 17   ○ 30   ○ 24   ○ 12   ○ none of these

5 Miguel takes a basket full of tennis balls out to practice hitting. The basket contains 20 orange, 10 yellow, 25 bright green, and 35 hot pink balls. Answer each of the following questions by writing a ratio.

a. Miguel reaches in, without looking, to grab a ball. What is the probability that he will get a ball that is not green?

b. Miguel did not get a green ball on his first pick. Now he grabs a second ball, without replacing the first one. What is the probability that this one will be green?

c. He replaces the first two balls and grabs two more without looking. What is the probability that both will be yellow?

Use ratios to show probability.

Do you know it? Show it:

1 Georgia tosses two coins at the same time. Write a ratio to show the probability of the result being two "heads."

2 The spinner is spun once.
What is the probability that the result will NOT be red (R)?

3 Nate is handed a pile of unlabeled envelopes. Each one contains a bill. Four envelopes hold a $50 bill; two hold $100s; and seven hold $20s. He is allowed to choose one envelope. What are the odds against his choosing an envelope with a $100 bill?

4 Five friends get in line for a movie, one behind the other. How many different possibilities exist for the order in which Abby, Ben, Chloe, Damian, and Evan can line up?

○ 120   ○ 15   ○ 60   ○ 25   ○ 15   ○ 200   ○ none of these

---

5  A basket of sandwiches is waiting for the chess players when they take a lunch break. There are three veggie sandwiches, five turkey, and ten roast beef. It's hard to tell the different kinds apart, because they are all covered in the same kind of wrapping.
Answer each of the following questions by writing a ratio.

a. MacKenzie grabs a sandwich. What is the probability that it will be turkey? _____

b. It turns out that she does get a turkey sandwich (and she eats it). Now Emma takes a sandwich. What is the probability that this, too, will be turkey? _____

c. Assume that MacKenzie reached into the full basket and grabbed a turkey sandwich, after which Emma grabbed a roast beef sandwich. What is the probability that Jamie, who grabbed a third sandwich, would get a veggie sandwich? _____

Write, solve, and graph inequalities.

Do you know it? Show it:

1 Tom's small sailboat is sinking fast. (It's lucky for Tom that he has a sturdy life raft.) The location of the sailboat at this point can be described this way:

*five more than twice the number of feet
is at most negative three*

Write an inequality to describe this situation. _____

2 Choose the graph of **x > (–2)**.

a.

b.

3 Solve the inequality: **x + 15 > 40**

4 Graph the inequality: **2x ≤ (–1)**.

---

5 Though Tom's prized sailboat sank (due to a gash in the side from a collision with a reef), he was able to find it and reclaim some of its equipment. Divers found the boat in a section of the bay on the grid below. That section is defined by the inequality:

$$y \leq 2x + 3$$

Other boats were found in the general area, but only one was located in that section. Graph the inequality to find that section.

Which boat is Tom's?

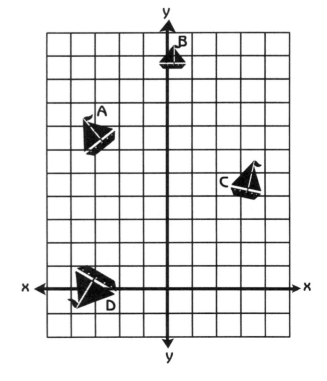

Write, solve, and graph inequalities.

Do you know it? Show it:

1 Four friends cruise several miles on a sunny Saturday afternoon. The distance can be described in this way.

negative four less than three times the distance
is greater than twenty-two

Write an inequality to describe this situation. _____

2 Solve the inequality: $\dfrac{-b}{4} \leq 2$

3 Choose the graph of $2x - 2 \leq x + 3$

a.

b.

4 Graph the inequality: $3 + x \geq -1$.

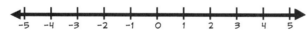

5 An afternoon outing turns into an adventure the friends did not anticipate. They are marooned on an island, waiting for rescue. The island is located entirely within the section of the grid described by this inequality.

$$x + 3y < 0$$

Graph the inequality to find that section.

On which island do they find themselves?

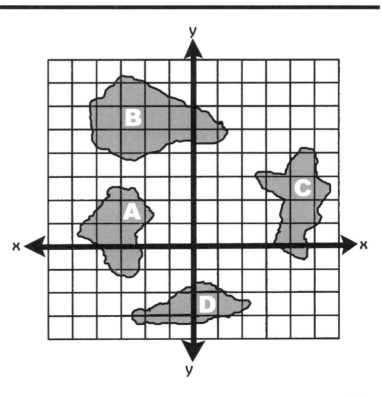

Solve equations with more than one variable.

Do you know it? Show it:

1. The difference between Caroline's age and the sum of Alicia's age and three times Brie's age is 25. If Alicia is ten and Caroline is half of Brie's age, how old are Caroline and Brie?

$$(a + 3b) - \tfrac{1}{2}b = 25$$

Caroline is _____   Brie is _____

2. In the problems below, which unknown variable has the greatest value?

a. Solve for y if x = –6. $\quad\quad -x^2 - 4y + y(x - 3) = 29$

b. Solve for n if k = –2 $\quad\quad 3k + n^2 - 20 = (-10)$

3. What is the product of $\tfrac{1}{4}x^2y$ and $\tfrac{1}{2}xy^4$?

○ $\tfrac{1}{6}x^2y^4$ ○ $\tfrac{1}{8}x^2y^4$ ○ $2x^8y^8$ ○ $\tfrac{3}{4}x^3y^5$ ○ $\tfrac{1}{8}x^3y^5$

4.
$$b^2 - 3c + d(b + c) = 75$$

a. In the equation above, if b = –10 and d = 2, what is c? _____

b. In the equation above, if b = 10 and d = 2, what is c? _____

---

5. The product of Jen's, Mario's, and Callie's ages is 120.
Jen is one-third of Mario's age. (The ages used are whole numbers.)

$$(j)(3j)(c) = 120$$

a. Assume that Callie is ten.
How old, then, is Mario? _____

b. If all three ages double, what
will happen to the product? _____

c. What age (besides ten)
might Callie be to make
the above statement true? _____

If I am ten, how old is Jen?

Solve equations with more than one variable.

Do you know it? Show it:

1 The square of Ryan's age is equal to the sum of Todd's and Antonio's ages. Todd is twice Antonio's age. If Ryan is six, how old are the others?

$$r^2 = 2a + a$$

Todd is _____   Antonio is _____

2 In the problems below, which unknown variable has the greatest value?

    a. Solve for n if p = –3 and q = 6. $p(q + 4) – 4n + p = (–25)$

    b. Solve for f if d = (–9) and c = (–4). $d + c^2 – 3f = 22$

3 What is the quotient of $\frac{1}{4}w^2x^3y^2$ and $\frac{2}{5}wxy^2$?

○ $\frac{9}{10}w^3x^4y^4$ ○ $\frac{9}{10}wx^2y$ ○ $\frac{5}{8}w^3x^4y^4$

○ $\frac{5}{8}wx^2y$ ○ $\frac{5}{8}wx^2$ ○ $\frac{8}{5}wx^2$

4
$$h^2 - 3g + g(2k - h) = 25$$

    a. In the equation above, if h = –2 and k = 4, what is g? _____

    b. In the equation above, if h = 1 and k = 3, what is g? _____

---

5 The relationship of Matt's, Nat's, and Pat's ages can be shown by this equation:

$$m - 2n - 3p = 18$$

    a. If Pat is 4 and Nat is 10, how old is Matt? _____

    b. If Nat's and Pat's ages are less, what will happen to Matt's age? _____

    c. If Matt's age is 34, what could Nat's and Pat's ages be? (Use only whole numbers.)

    Nat _____ Pat _____

Compare geometric figures.

Do you know it? Show it:

1

A sign that is congruent to this one will have a base measurement of
○ 5 in   ○ 10 in   ○ 20 in   ○ 1 in   ○ none of these

2
Kayla's cylindrical water bottle has a diameter of 9 cm and a height of 21 cm. Zach has a bottle that is a similar figure. Its radius is 6 cm. What is its height?

3
The angle at the bottom left vertex of an isosceles trapezoid measures 45°. What is the measure of the angle inside the top right vertex?

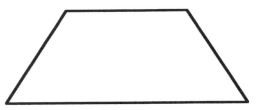

4
In the figure to the right, if m ∠ 4 is 140°, what is m ∠ 5?

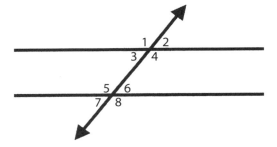

5
This figure represents the tent's actual size drawn to scale.

a. The tent is actually 49 inches tall. What is the scale of the drawing?

b. What is the actual length of the top long edge of the tent?

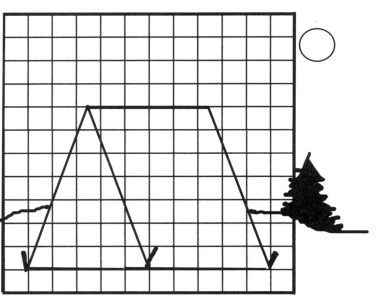

Compare geometric figures.

Do you know it? Show it:

1. A sign that is similar to this one with a bottom base of 3.5 in will have a top base measuring

○ 16.5 in   ○ 22 in   ○ 7.5 in   ○ none of these

2. Luke's tent has a height of 60 in, a length of 84 in, and a width of 48 in. Tyson's tent is a similar figure with a width of 36 in. What is its height?

3.  The angle inside the top left vertex of a regular hexagon measures 120°. What is the measure of the angle inside the bottom right vertex?

4. In the figure to the right, if m ∠ 7 is 40°, what is m ∠ 1?

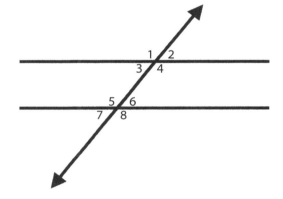

5. This figure represents the actual size of the bear drawn to scale.

The bear is actually 24 in wide at the widest spot in the picture.

a. What is the scale?

b. What is the bear's height?

27a Use formulas to find area and volume of figures.

Do you know it? Show it:

1 Which of the following signs has the greatest area?

A 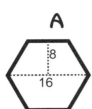   B 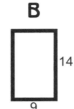   C 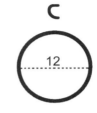   D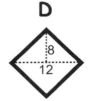

2 The volume of a cylinder is 1004.8 cm^3. Its height is 20 cm. What is the diameter?

3 Which figure has a surface area closest to that of the sphere? (Circle the figure.)

   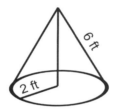   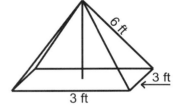

r = 3 ft

4 What is the difference between the volume of the two figures described?

- a triangular prism with a height of 15 cm and a base with dimensions of b = 10 cm and h = 12 cm _____

   AND

- a square pyramid with a height of 14 cm and a base with dimensions s = 12 _____

5 A sandwich board sign is the same size and shape on both pieces. Each piece is a thin regular rectangular prism. The dimensions are: 3.5 ft tall, 2 ft wide, and 0.2 ft thick.

Suzannah wants to paint all the large surfaces of the sign with bright orange paint. She will paint the skinny edges with hot pink paint. The paint comes in relatively small bottles, and each bottle covers just $2\frac{1}{2}$ sq ft. How much paint will she need to buy?

a. orange _____   b. pink _____

27b Use formulas to find area and volume of figures.

Do you know it? Show it:

1 Which of the following signs has the smallest area?

A   B 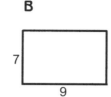 C 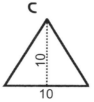 D

2 The volume of a square pyramid is 8,800 ft³. Its height is 22 ft. What is the area of its base?

3 Which figure has a surface area closest to that of the cylinder? (Circle the figure.)

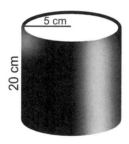 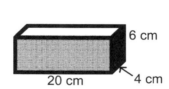 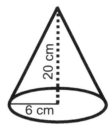

4 What is the difference between the volume of the two figures? (Round to the nearest whole number.)

- a cylinder with a height of 6 m and a radius of 2 m
  AND
- a sphere with a diameter of 6 m

5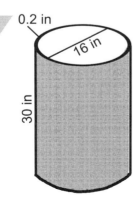

Justin is preparing a canister to keep snorkel equipment. He needs to have something waterproof. So he gets a cylindrical wastebasket and covers it, inside and out, with an adhesive plastic. The wastebasket is 30 in tall and has a 16-in diameter across the bottom to the outside edge. The "walls" of the wastebasket are 0.2 in thick. He will not need to cover the rim of the wastebasket.

How much plastic will he need to cover the outside (including the bottom)? _____

Will it take the same amount of plastic to cover the inside? ____
Why or why not? _____

Recognize and use relationships in right triangles.

Do you know it? Show it:

1 Lauren jogs every day on the path shown. She's getting some strain on her knees. Maybe it's from the sharp turns at the vertices of this triangular path! What is the angle at pond end of the path?

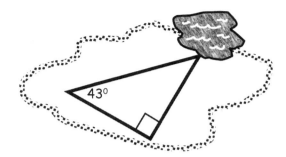

2 The hypotenuse of a triangle is 30 cm long and the length of leg A is 15 cm. How long is leg B? (Round to the nearest tenth.)

○ 15 cm   ○ 26 cm   ○ 25 cm   ○ 25.3 cm   ○ none of these

3 Find the distance between **(–4, 8)** and **(10, –5)**. Round to the nearest tenth.

a. 19.1 units   c. 15 units   e. 13 units
b. 9 units   d. 25.1 units   f. 18.9 units

4 In a right triangle, side A = $xy + 3z$ and side B = $xy + 4z$. What is the length of side C, the hypotenuse?

a. $2x^2y^2 + 25z^2$ c. $\sqrt{2x^2y^2 + 7xy^2 + 25z^2}$
b. $2xy^2 + 7z$ d. none of these

5 Stephanie is biking to a basketball game. She always takes the shortcut through the parking lot of a sporting goods store. This route is just 1 mi long from her house to the school.

Today, however, that path is blocked because the lot is being repaved. Therefore, she goes a distance of .8 mi along Greene Street and another distance **x** along Browne Avenue, making a sharp right angle turn onto Browne.

How much farther is this route than her shortcut?

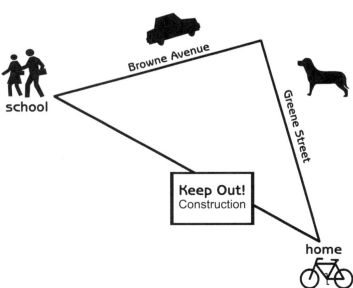

28b Recognize and use relationships in right triangles.

Do you know it? Show it:

1.
Lucy swims in a triangular pattern every morning. She takes sharp turns at the vertices of the triangular path. The angle inside B is 30°. What is the angle of her turn at C?

2. If the hypotenuse (leg C) of a triangle is 40 m long and the length of leg A is 23 m. How long is leg B? (Round to the nearest tenth.)

  ○ 32.7 m   ○ 46.1 m   ○ 30 m   ○ 4.1 m   ○ none of these

3. Find the distance between **(6, –6)** and **(–9, 3)**. Round to the nearest tenth.

  a. 9 units   c. 15 units   e. 17.5 units
  b. 24 units   d. 36.6 units   f. 6 units

4. In a right triangle, side A = 4ab + 3 and side B = 3ab + 4. What is the length of side C, the hypotenuse?

  a. $16a^2b^2 + 9a^2b^2 + 7$ c. $16a^2b^2 + 9a^2b^2 + 25$ e. $5ab + 5$
  b. $\sqrt{25a^2b^2 + 24ab + 25}$ d. $5ab + 5$ f. none of these

---

5. Bradley's paper route includes 20 customers. The last three customers each live a long distance from anyone else. Mr. G, Ms. T, and the C family live at the corners of a right triangle. Recently Ms. T dropped her subscription. Now, instead of riding from G to T to C, Bradley can travel directly to C. Each tenth of a mile on his route takes him 1.5 minutes to ride, given the hilly terrain and his heavy load.

How much time will Brad save now that he can take a shorter route from Mr. G's to the Cs' home?

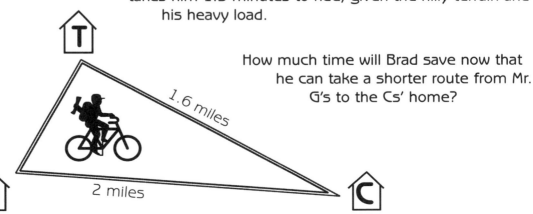

Graph number pairs on a coordinate grid.

Do you know it? Show it:

1 A four-quadrant grid lies on a section of the ocean floor. Three crabs rest on the grid. One is at (–3, –5). The second is at (4, –8). The third is at (–6, 7). How many are in the first quadrant?

2 Which number pair has a point on the y-axis?
  (0, –4)   (5, 5)   (1, –1)   (–9, 0)

3 Find the crab on the grid below. Write its location.

4 On the grid below, name the creature or object found at each coordinate pair.
  a. (–6, –3) _____   c. (0, –3) _____
  b. (9, –2) _____   d. (5, –5) _____

5 Follow the instructions to draw the following items onto the grid.
  a. Draw a shell at (–6, 0).
  b. Draw a fish at (–8, 5).
  c. Draw an octopus that extends into the first, third, and fourth quadrants.

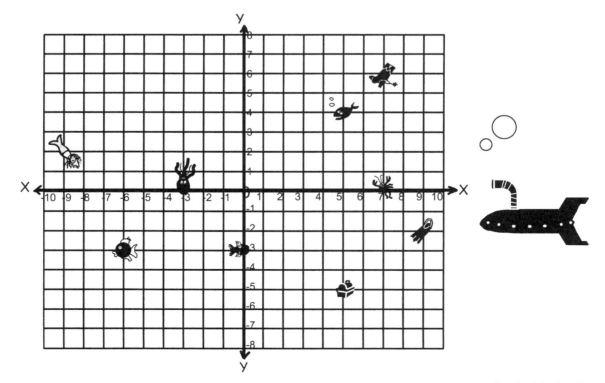

Graph number pairs on a coordinate grid.

Do you know it? Show it:

1. A four-quadrant grid lies on a section of the ocean floor. Four submarines hover above the grid. Their locations are: (–20, 4); (0, 12); (–7, –3); and (–18, 4). How many are in the second quadrant?

2. Which number pair has a point below the x-axis?

(–5, 0)   (4, –6)   (–9, 6)   (7, 4)

---

3. Find Submarine A on the grid below. Write its location.

4. On the grid below, name the object found at each coordinate pair.

a. (–3, 0) _____   c. (–6, –4) _____

b. (6, –4) _____   d. (4, 5) _____

5. Follow the instructions to draw the following items onto the grid.

a. Draw a fish at (0, –4).

b. Draw a bubble at (–5, –6).

c. Draw an eel that extends into the second and third quadrants.

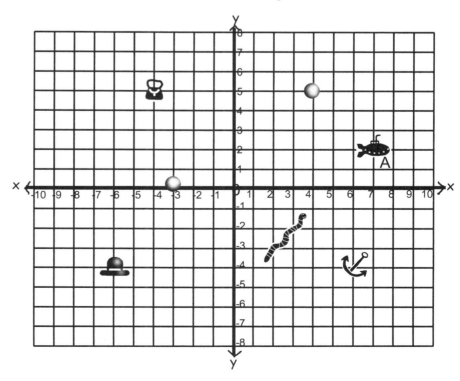

Plot transformations of figures on a grid.

Do you know it? Show it:

1 Which example shows a reflection (flip) of the first figure?

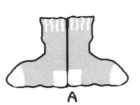

2 Draw a 180° turn of this figure around point X.

3 A figure has vertices B (2, 6), C (–6, –3), and D (–2, –4). Find the coordinates of D after the figure is rotated 90° clockwise around vertex B.

(4, –2)   (–2, 4)   (2, 16)   (–8, 10)   (–2, 6)

4 A figure with vertices W (–2, 3), X (5, 4), Y (7, –2), and Z (–4, –7) slides negative two on the x-axis and positive two on the y-axis. Where is vertex Z after the slide?

_____

5 Anya was given the following figure (solid line) with instructions to flip the figure across the y-axis. Her figure is the one with the dotted lines.

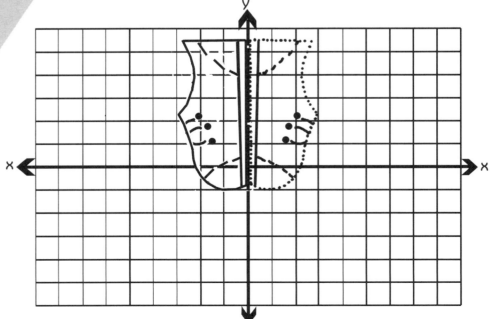

Did she get it right? _____

(If not, explain what she did wrong.)

Plot transformations of figures on a grid.

Do you know it? Show it:

1 Which example shows a translation (slide) of the first figure?

2 Draw a flip of the following figure across the axis.

3 A figure has vertices X (7, –7), Y (1, 2), and Z (–8, 4). Find the coordinates of Y after a slide of the figure three right on the x-axis and four down on the y-axis.

(4, –2)   (–2, 4)   (2, 16)   (–8, 6)   (–2, 6)

4 A figure with vertices P (–1, 6), Q (5, 4), and R (0, –5) reflects (flips) horizontally from left to right. Where is vertex Q after the flip?

_____

5 Alex was given the following figure (solid line) with instructions to rotate the figure 270° clockwise around the B vertex. His figure is the one with the dotted lines.

Did he get it right? _____

(If not, explain what he did wrong.)

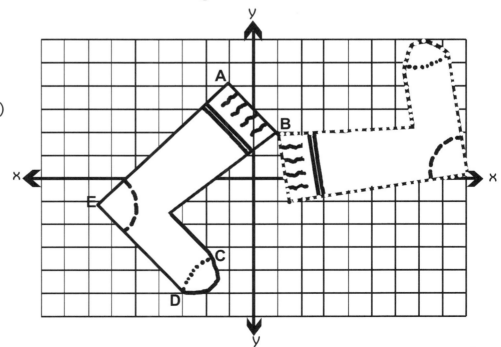

I've Got It!—Pre-Algebra Skills
Copyright ©2008 by Incentive Publications, Inc., Nashville, TN.

Identify and describe functions.

Do you know it? Show it:

1 A math student made these statements about functions. Circle the letters of those that are true.

a. A function is an equation.
b. For any one value of x in a function, there are at least two values of y.
c. A function may be written in this form: $y = mx + b$.
d. A function always has a straight line as a graph.
e. When a function is graphed, a vertical line drawn through a point does not pass through any other points.

2 Which relation is a function?
   a. {(–5, –4), (3, 2) (4, –4), (5, 2), (–1, 3)}
   b. {(–3, –7), (0, –4), (2, –2), (–2, –6), (3, –1)}
   c. {(–4, –1), (4, –1) (3, –2), (–3, –2), (–1, 1)}
   d. {(6, 0), (5, 1) (4, 2), (3, 0), (2, 1)}

3 Is this a graph of a function? _____

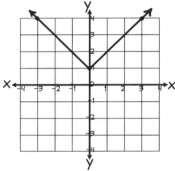

4 Identify which numbers represent the domain of the pairs.
   {(–3, –7), (–1, –5), (0, –4), (3, –1), (4, 0)} _____

5 Complete the table. Then graph the equation.

y = 2x - 1		
x	y	(x, y)
-2		
-1		
0		
1		
2		

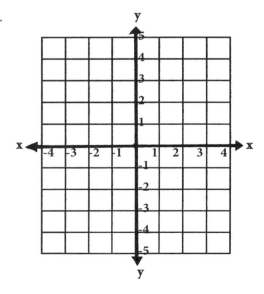

Is this a function? _____
How can you tell?
_____
_____

Identify and describe functions.

Do you know it? Show it:

1. A math student made these statements about functions. Circle the letters of those that are true.

   a. A function may take this form: $y = mx^3 + b$
   b. For any one value of x in a function, there is only one value of y.
   c. A function is an equation.
   d. A function may graph as a curved line.
   e. When a function is graphed, a vertical line drawn through a point does not pass through any other points.

2. Which relation is a function?
   a. {(–6, –8), (4, –6) (4, –4), (2, 0), (2, 2), (2, 4)}
   b. {(–7, –3), (–4, 0), (–2, 2), (–6, –2), (–1, 3)}
   c. {(–1, –4), (–1, 4) (–2, 3), (–3, –2), (1, –1)}
   d. {(–11, –3), (–8, –2) (–2, 0), (1, 1), (–2, 3), (16, 6}

3. Is this a graph of a function? _____

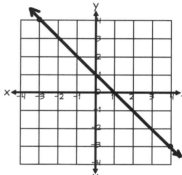

4. Identify which numbers represent the range of the pairs.
   {(–3, –7), (–1, –5), (0, –4), (3, –1), (4, 0)} _____

5. Complete the table. Then graph the equation.

y + 1 = 3x		
x	y	(x, y)
-2		
-1		
0		
1		
2		

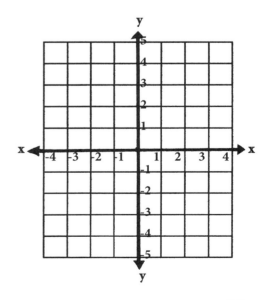

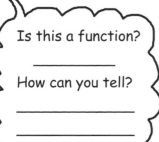

Is this a function? _____
How can you tell?
_____
_____

Identify and graph linear equations.

Do you know it? Show it:

1 An airplane flies the courses described by the equations below that are linear. Which equations can be graphed as a line?

    A. $3x + 2y = 10$ C. $y - 4 = 2x$ E. $y = x^2 + 4$

    B. $x + \frac{6}{y} = 12$ D. $-y = 4x$ F. $2xy + y = -2$

2 Which example (below) is a graph of **y = x + 2**? _____

                        What is the slope? _____

3 Which example (below) is a graph of **y = 2x + 1**? _____

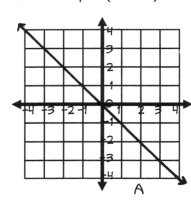
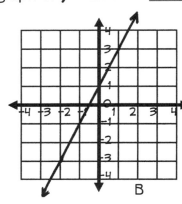
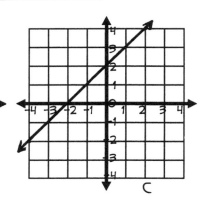

        A   B   C

4 A line passes through (–4, 4) and (2, –2).

    a. What is the rise? _____

    b. What is the run? _____

5 Graph the following line:
    x – y + 1 = 0

Write the equation in slope-intercept form.

_____

Identify and graph linear equations.

Do you know it? Show it:

1 A helicopter flies a course that follows a line. Which of these are linear equations and thus could represent a flight path?

   A. $y = x^2 - 2$ C. $2x + y = 8$ E. $y - 1 = 2x$

   B. $-y = x$ D. $x + \frac{3}{y} = 6$ F. $y - xy = 3$

2 Which example (below) is a graph of **x − 3 = y**? _____
What is the slope? _____

3 Which example (below) is a graph of **y = −x + 5**? _____

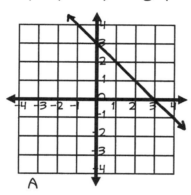
A

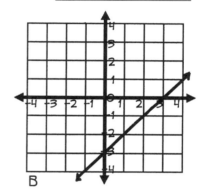
B

4 A line passes through (4, −1) and (0, 3).

   a. What is the rise? _____

   b. What is the run? _____

5 Graph the following line:
−2x + 3 = −y

Write the equation in slope-intercept form.

_____

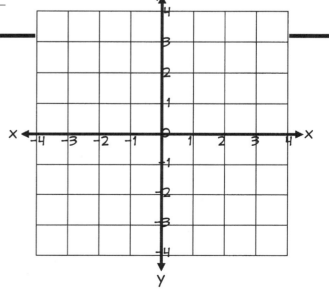

Determine features of linear equations.

33a

Do you know it? Show it:

1. Julianna stands at the top of a steep ski hill, ready to push off and head down the slope. Is she embarking on a negative or positive slope?

2. Give the slope of each line.

   a. $x - y = -2$ c. $4x - 5y = 0$

   b. $3x + 20 = -4y$ d. $y = -1$

3. A line passes through $(-3, 5)$ and $(4, 6)$. What is its slope? _____

4. Which is the equation of a line that is parallel to $-x - 2y = -2$ and passes through $(1, -10)$?

   ○ $x + 2y = -19$ ○ $x - 2y = -9$ ○ $x + 2y = -12$

5. $y = \frac{-2x}{3} - 2$

   a. What is the y-intercept of this line (equation above)? _____

   b. What is the slope of the above line? _____

   c. Graph the line. Which skier is following this line? _____

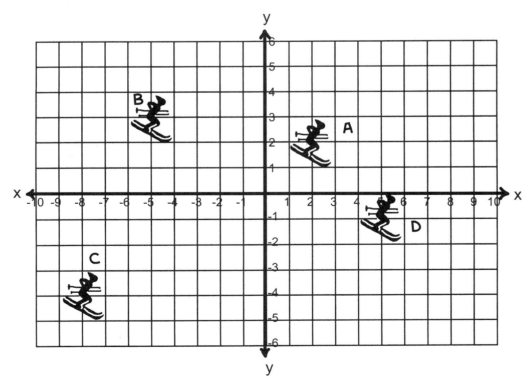

Determine features of linear equations.

Do you know it? Show it:

1 Jamie takes off on her skis, heading on a straight-line course. Her path is plotted on a grid. She moves from left to right on a slope of $2\frac{1}{2}$. Derek tackles the hill on his snowboard, heading on a left to right straight-line course that has a slope of –2. Which skier is going downhill?

2 Give the slope of each line.

a. $-15 - x = -5y$ c. $y = -x + 3$

b. $y = 4x - 1$ d. $y = x - 1$

3 What is the y-intercept of this line: $4x - 2y = 6$? _____

4 A line passes through points (–5, 2) and (2, –3).

a. What is its slope? _____   b. What is the y-intercept? _____

5 $y + 3x = 5$

a. Graph the line (equation above). Which boarder is following this line? _____

b. What is the y-intercept of this line? _____

c. What is the slope of the above line? _____

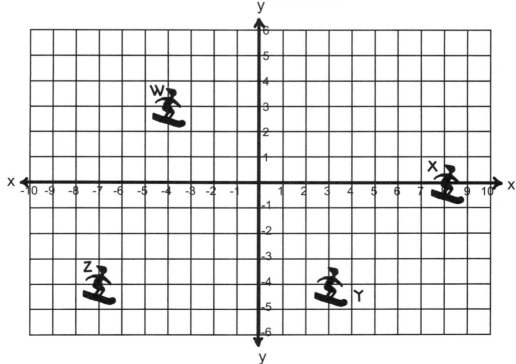

Identify and operate with polynomials.

Do you know it? Show it:

1 Pedro's pet parrot is a brilliant mathematician. Her name is Polly (what a surprise!) and she is quite proficient with polynomials. In fact, she is so particular that she will ONLY do math tasks that include polynomials. Which of these will she bother to work? Circle and simplify the polynomials.

A. $3ab^2 + ab - c - ab$

B. $6x - xy + 3x + x^2$

C. $(24\,abc \div 6abc) + 2abc$

D. $xyz - 14$

2 Find the sum: $(6rs - w^2 + t) + (3rs + w^2 - t) =$

3 Polly is proud of her factoring abilities. She has dictated three sets of factors.

a. $(3x + 3)(3x + y + 3)$ b. $(2y)(4x + 3xy + 1)$ c. $(3x)(3x^2 + y + 9)$

A. Which are factors of $9x^3 + 3xy + 27x$?

                                    a.   b.   c.   none of these

B. Which are factors of $8xy + 6xy + 2y$?

                                    a.   b.   c.   none of these

4 Find the product. $(3x^2 - 6)(4y + xy) =$ _____

5 Polly's spacious cage is a regular rectangular prism. The length exceeds the width by 30 cm and the height is 20 cm more than the width. The total area of the 4 walls exceeds the area of the floor and top together by 13,200. What are the dimensions of the cage?

    a. 50 cm x 70 cm x 80 cm

    b. 100 cm x 70 cm x 50 cm

    c. 110 cm x 60 cm x 80 cm

    d. 80 cm x 60 cm x 90 cm

    e. none of these

Identify and operate with polynomials.

Do you know it? Show it:

1. Patricia's pet parrot not only talks constantly, but spouts math facts easily, too. Pollyanna loves long algebraic expressions, particularly polynomials. Which of the following fit that description?
Circle and simplify the polynomials.

   A. $12p - 3pq + 3p - 2pq + q^2$

   B. $9def - 4def + 12def$

   C. $10xy^2 + xy - x - xy$

   D. $(24\,abc \div 6abc) + 2abc$

2. Find the sum: $(7x^3 + y) + (9y - 4x^3 - 12 + y) =$

3. Pollyanna is proud of her factoring abilities. She has dictated three sets of factors.
   a. $(5a + 7 + 2)(6ab - 4)$ b. $(2b)(15a + b - 18)$ c. $(b)(30a^2 + b - 36)$

   A. Which are factors of $30a^2b - 20a + 54\,ab - 36$?

                                       a.   b.   c.   none of these

   B. Which are factors of $30ab + 2b^2 - 36b$?

                                       a.   b.   c.   none of these

4. Find the product. $(7a^2b^2 - 5)(a^2b^2 + 5) =$ _____

---

5. Patricia's pet parrot, Pollyanna, chatters all the time. She speaks 150 words a day more than Pedro's pet parrot, Polly. Together these parrots speak 1,722 words in a week (7 days).

How many words does Pollyanna speak in three days?

   a. 1050

   b. 758

   c. 288

   d. 450

   e. 738

   f. none of these

Use algebra to solve a variety of problems.

Do you know it? Show it:

1 The ages of four kayakers are consecutive even numbers. Trent, the oldest, is one and three-eighths the age of the youngest, Tyler. How old is Trent?

Write and solve an equation to answer the question.

2 Using his powerful electric pump, Jason can blow up his raft in 40 minutes. Erik can blow up the same raft with his mechanical foot pump, but it takes 60 minutes. Working with both pumps and two separate valves, they can blow up the raft together. How long will this take?

      a. 120 min   c. 60 min   e. 20 min

      b. 24 min   d. 34 min   f. none of these

3 A river flows downstream at 1 mph. A canoer paddles upstream at 5 mph for a distance of 20 miles. How long does this take?

Write and solve an equation to answer the question.

4 Some friends began an outing in their sea kayaks with a morning wind of 6 mph. By the end of the day, the wind speed measured 33 mph. What was the rate of change? (Give the answer as a percent.)

---

5 Samantha gets familiar with her kayak by paddling around a neighborhood pool. The pool has an even depth. It is 38 ft wide and 60 ft long. The pool is filled to a line just one foot below the top edge and has 20,520 cu ft of water in it.

    a. What is the depth of the pool (to the top edge—one foot above the water line)? _____

    b. One side wall (length) is painted red. The other side wall and end walls (width) are painted blue. If the red wall is painted only to the waterline, what is the area of the red portion of the wall? _____

Use algebra to solve a variety of problems.

Do you know it? Show it:

1. Friends Charlie, Derek, and Emmie have each won several kayak competitions. The numbers they have won are consecutive odd numbers. Emmie's wins are nine fewer than twice Charlie's. (Charlie has the least wins of the three friends. Emmie has the most.) How many competitions has Derek won?

Write and solve an equation to answer the question.

2. Chaundra canoes 10 hours over a 60-mile course. She turns around and heads back on the same course. The trip back takes six hours. What is her average speed for the trip?

  a. 12 mph   c. 6 mph   e. 6.5 mph   g. 7.5 mph
  b. 24 mph   d. 10 mph   f. 18 mph   h. none of these

3. Max practices his kayaking skills 78 hours in six weeks. Write and solve a proportion to find the number of weeks it would take (at the same rate) to have practiced 234 hours.

4. At the end of a rafting competition, the winner gets to choose two envelopes from a basket of unmarked envelopes. Each envelope holds an amount of money. Nine envelopes hold $50, four hold $100, and three hold $500. Winner Tracy takes two envelopes. What is the probability that both envelopes will hold $500?

5. Two lines are graphed. Each represents the path of a canoe on a river.
The path for Canoe A is a line that passes through (−2, 3) and (5, 4).
The path for Canoe B is a line that passes through (−4, 1) and (1, −5).

  a. Which canoe has the steepest route? _____

  b. What is the slope of route A? _____

  c. What is the slope of route B? _____

Pre-Algebra End-of-Course Tasks
Student Record Sheet

NAME

Task		Part **a**, date and # correct	Part **b**, date and # correct
1	Recognize and define numbers and number systems.		
2	Compare and order numbers.		
3	Recognize and use properties of numbers and operations.		
4	Recognize and use order of operations.		
5	Perform operations with positive and negative numbers.		
6	Identify elements of mathematical expressions.		
7	Read and write expressions.		
8	Simplify and evaluate expressions.		
9	Evaluate expressions with radicals and exponents.		
10	Perform operations with radicals and exponents.		
11	Recognize and use factors and multiples.		
12	Perform operations with fractions and decimals.		
13	Solve problems with percent.		
14	Factor expressions and equations.		
15	Translate problems into equations.		
16	Solve equations using inverse operations.		
17	Solve equations with one variable and one step.		
18	Solve multi-step equations.		
19	Solve equations with rational numbers.		
20	Solve equations with radicals and exponents.		
21	Find rate, time, and distance.		
22	Solve problems with ratio and proportion.		
23	Use ratios to show probability.		
24	Write, solve, and graph inequalities.		
25	Solve equations with more than one variable.		
26	Compare geometric figures.		
27	Use formulas to find area and volume of figures.		
28	Recognize and use relationships in right triangles.		
29	Graph number pairs on a coordinate grid.		
30	Plot transformations of figures on a grid.		
31	Identify and describe functions.		
32	Identify and graph linear equations.		
33	Determine features of linear equations.		
34	Identify and operate with polynomials.		
35	Use algebra to solve a variety of problems.		

Putting It All Together, Cumulative Review (pgs 86–91) Date _____ Score _____ of 65

Pre-Algebra End-of-Course Tasks, Class Record Sheet

Class _____   Teacher _____

Tasks: Write # of items correct for Part a and Part b of each task

	1	2	3	4	5	6	7	8	9	10	11	12	13	14	15	16	17	18	19	20	21	22	23	24	25	26	27	28	29	30	31	32	33	34	35
Name	a	a	a	a	a	a	a	a	a	a	a	a	a	a	a	a	a	a	a	a	a	a	a	a	a	a	a	a	a	a	a	a	a	a	a
C.R. Score	b	b	b	b	b	b	b	b	b	b	b	b	b	b	b	b	b	b	b	b	b	b	b	b	b	b	b	b	b	b	b	b	b	b	b
Name	a	a	a	a	a	a	a	a	a	a	a	a	a	a	a	a	a	a	a	a	a	a	a	a	a	a	a	a	a	a	a	a	a	a	a
C.R. Score	b	b	b	b	b	b	b	b	b	b	b	b	b	b	b	b	b	b	b	b	b	b	b	b	b	b	b	b	b	b	b	b	b	b	b
Name	a	a	a	a	a	a	a	a	a	a	a	a	a	a	a	a	a	a	a	a	a	a	a	a	a	a	a	a	a	a	a	a	a	a	a
C.R. Score	b	b	b	b	b	b	b	b	b	b	b	b	b	b	b	b	b	b	b	b	b	b	b	b	b	b	b	b	b	b	b	b	b	b	b
Name	a	a	a	a	a	a	a	a	a	a	a	a	a	a	a	a	a	a	a	a	a	a	a	a	a	a	a	a	a	a	a	a	a	a	a
C.R. Score	b	b	b	b	b	b	b	b	b	b	b	b	b	b	b	b	b	b	b	b	b	b	b	b	b	b	b	b	b	b	b	b	b	b	b
Name	a	a	a	a	a	a	a	a	a	a	a	a	a	a	a	a	a	a	a	a	a	a	a	a	a	a	a	a	a	a	a	a	a	a	a
C.R. Score	b	b	b	b	b	b	b	b	b	b	b	b	b	b	b	b	b	b	b	b	b	b	b	b	b	b	b	b	b	b	b	b	b	b	b
Name	a	a	a	a	a	a	a	a	a	a	a	a	a	a	a	a	a	a	a	a	a	a	a	a	a	a	a	a	a	a	a	a	a	a	a
C.R. Score	b	b	b	b	b	b	b	b	b	b	b	b	b	b	b	b	b	b	b	b	b	b	b	b	b	b	b	b	b	b	b	b	b	b	b
Name	a	a	a	a	a	a	a	a	a	a	a	a	a	a	a	a	a	a	a	a	a	a	a	a	a	a	a	a	a	a	a	a	a	a	a
C.R. Score	b	b	b	b	b	b	b	b	b	b	b	b	b	b	b	b	b	b	b	b	b	b	b	b	b	b	b	b	b	b	b	b	b	b	b

Duplicate this chart as needed to include all students.

C.R. is Cumulative Review on pages 86–91, total score possible is 65.

Putting It All Together

For questions 1–20, compare the quantities given in A and B.
Circle A if the quantity represented by A is greater than (>) the quantity represented by B.
Circle B if the quantity represented by B is greater than (>) the quantity represented by A.
Circle E if the quantities are equal.
Circle N if there is not enough information for you to decide.

1 x and y are integers.
  $-4x + 6y = 48$
  A) x
  B) y
  E   N

2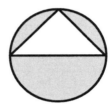
  A) $2\frac{1}{2}$ times area of triangle
  B) area of the circle
  E   N

3 A) 45% of 32
  B) 38% of 45
  E   N

4 Train A travels 1,037.5 mi in 12.5 hours.
  Train B travels 581 mi in 7 hours.
  A) Train A's average speed (rate)
  B) Train B's average speed (rate)
  E   N

5 A) $\frac{3}{5} \div \frac{4}{6}$
  B) $\frac{2}{3} \cdot \frac{4}{5}$
  E   N

6 A cube has a side measuring 5 cm.
  A sphere has a diameter of 6 cm.
  A) the cube's volume
  B) the sphere's volume
  E   N

7 A) slope of line: $3y = -9x + 12$
  B) slope of line: $2y = -6x + 4$
  E   N

8 x is a negative integer.
  A) $\frac{7}{9}x$
  B) $\frac{4}{5}x$
  E   N

9 Factory X made 126,000 chocolate kisses in March. In April, there was a 280% increase in production.
  Factory Z made 500,000 kisses in March and had a 15% product decrease in April.
  A) number of kisses produced in April in Factory Z
  B) number of kisses produced in April in Factory X
  E   N

86
I've Got It!—Pre-Algebra Skills
Copyright ©2008 by Incentive Publications, Inc., Nashville, TN.

Putting It All Together

Circle A if the quantity represented by A is greater than (>) the quantity represented by B.
Circle B if the quantity represented by B is greater than (>) the quantity represented by A.
Circle E if the quantities are equal.
Circle N if there is not enough information for you to decide.

10 A) $(4 \cdot 5) - 8(4 \div 2)$
B) $4(5 - 8) \cdot (4 \div 2)$
E N

11 A) $(x^2 \div x^{-5})$ B) $(x^{-4} \cdot x^{-3})$
E N

12 A) $x - 2 \geq -6$ B) $x + 5 < -4$
E N

13 A) 4^{-3} B) 2^{-6}
E N

14  1   2

A) $m\angle A + m\angle B$ in figure 1
B) $m\angle W + m\angle Y$ in figure 2
E N

15 A) the y-intercept of a straight line on a coordinate plane passing through $(-1, 1)$ and $(1, 5)$
B) the y-intercept of a straight line in a coordinate plane passing through $(-7, 8)$ and $(2, -6)$
E N

16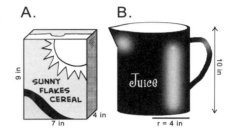

A) surface area of cereal box
B) surface area of juice container
E N

17 x is the same in both A and B
A) value of x in $4x^2 - x^2 + 3x - 4$
B) value of x in $x(x^2 + 2) - x + 7$
E N

18 Alex has six shoes of different colors spread across the floor.
A) number of combinations of two shoes that he could choose
B) number of permutations for the order of the shoes on the floor
E N

19 A) the absolute value of $-3x$
B) the opposite of y
E N

20 A) the value of n in $\frac{2}{3}n = \frac{1}{2}$
B) the value of n in $\frac{3}{4}n = \frac{1}{3}$
E N

Putting It All Together

21 Miguel has a mix-up of single socks in his drawer. There are 6 black, 4 white, 7 green, 3 blue, and 4 red socks. He reaches in, without looking, and grabs two socks. What is the probability that he will get a pair of white socks?

$\frac{2}{6}$ $\frac{1}{12}$

$\frac{1}{46}$ $\frac{2}{24}$

22 Evaluate the following expression if $x = 2$ and $y = -4$.

$x^3 + (x - y)^2 + 3xy =$

23 Julia can clean a full pail of fish in 80 minutes. Vicki can clean the same pail of fish in 2 hours. Working together, how long will it take them to clean the pail of fish?

a. 40 min   c. 160 min
b. 48 min   d. 100 min

24 Is this a graph of $\frac{1}{2}x \geq 3$? _____

25 Circle the letters of equations that are correctly solved.

a. $\frac{2}{3}g = \frac{1}{2}$ $g = \frac{3}{4}$

b. $-9t - 14 = 4$ $t = -2$

c. $8n + n(-5) = 30$ $n = -10$

26 What is the greatest common factor of $8a^2b + 12a^2 + 2ab^2 - 6a$?

27 16% of what number is 12?

28 $9a^2b^3 - 3a^2b$ is equivalent to which of the following?

a. $6a^2 - b^2$ c. $3(a^2b^3)$
b. $3a^2(3ab^3)$ d. $3a^2(3b^3 - b)$

29 Spider A crawled to the web by traveling from XY to YX. Spider B got to the web by crawling from X directly to Z.

How much farther did A crawl than B?

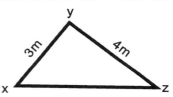

30 What is -14 decreased by -20?

31 What object is located on the grid at $(-4, 2)$?

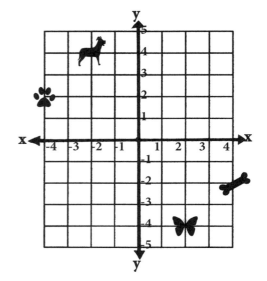

Putting It All Together

32 The sum of
2n + 8 + 6n + 8
is how much greater than n?

33 Evaluate the expression
a − (−b) + (a − c)
when a = 4, b = −2, and c = −5

34 Jennifer and Jamie watched the new pirate movie five times in eight consecutive days. If they continue watching at this rate, in what week will they watch it the hundredth time?

35 Which example matches these words?
three times the difference between the square of a number and the cube of another number

  a. $3(x^2 - y^3)$ c. $(x^2 - y^3)$
  b. $3x^2 - y^3$ d. $\frac{1}{2}x^2 + y^3$

36 Circle the letters of examples that are correctly simplified.
  a. $6 + x(3 - 7) + 8 = 14 - 4x$
  b. $-4\sqrt{125} + 13 = 7$
  c. $4m + 7n - n(3 + 6n) + 5m = 9m - 6n^2$
  d. $\sqrt{242} + \sqrt{16}\,x = 11\sqrt{2} + 4x$

37 What is 325% of 72?

38 Luke's duffle bag is a similar figure to this one. His bag is 18 inches long. What is the height of Luke's bag?

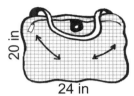

39 Solve: $(-4)(6) + (-15 \div -5) =$

40 The figure below, when placed on a coordinate plane, has vertices at the following points: A at (−6, 1); B at (1, 1); C at (1, −6); and D at (−7, −2). When the figure is flipped vertically across line AB, what is the new location of vertex D?

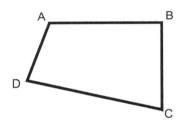

41 What is the negative solution to:
$x^2 - x + 5 = 25$?

42 Write 0.138 in scientific notation.

43 A river flows 2 mph downstream. A canoer paddles upstream at 5 mph for a distance of 12 miles. How long does this take?

Putting It All Together

44 Write $\frac{7}{15}$ as a decimal rounded to the nearest hundredth.

45 Apply the distributive property:
$-3x(2x + 3y + 9)$

46 Is this a graph of a function?

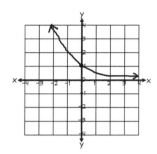

47 Solve: $12 + 3x \leq -6$

48 Choose the equation that can be used to solve the problem below.

Chad is twice Brad's age.

Tad is twice Chad's age.

The sum of their ages is 42.

How old is Chad?

a. $\frac{1}{2}c + c + 2c = 42$
b. $b + 2b + 2(b + 2b) = 42$
c. $b + 2b + 4b = 42$

49 Evaluate pq when $p = -33.5$ and $q = 4.2$.

50 Is this a graph of $x = -y$?

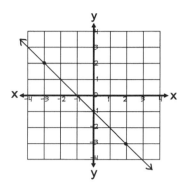

51 Some pirate friends stashed a supply of gold coins in a hidden island cave. Pirate Pete picked up $\frac{1}{2}$ of the coins. Lulu picked up $\frac{1}{3}$ of the original supply of coins the next day. Jake took $\frac{2}{5}$ of the remaining coins at midnight. When Black Bart arrived, there were 75,000 coins left. How many coins were originally stashed in the cave?

52 144 is what percent of 400?

53 This is a graph of which inequality? (Circle the letter of the answer.)

a. $2x \geq 3 - 7$
b. $2x > 3 - 7$
c. $x \leq -2$
d. $4 - 3x > -3$

54 A line passes through points $(-3, 2)$ and $(7, -8)$ on a coordinate plane. What is the rise?

Putting It All Together

55 268 is 335% of what number?

56 What is the slope of the hill (line) that the skier is following?

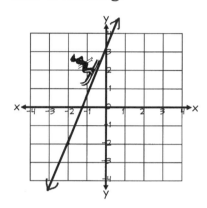

57 Are these numbers in order from least to greatest value?

-3^5; 2^7; 1.26; $\frac{14}{8}$; π; 3.15; 2.6×10^2; $\sqrt{225}$

58 Which number pair would be found in the fourth quadrant of a coordinate grid?

(0, –8); (4, 7); (–2, –4); (–5, 5); (3, –2); (–4, 0)

59 Gabe has a suitcase that measures 24 in x 8 in x 16 in. He wants to use it to transport a jellybean collection. Right now, the jellybeans fill a cylindrical wastebasket that has a 28-in height and a 10-in diameter. Will the jellybeans fit in the suitcase?

60 If the volume of a pyramid with a 5-meter square base is 50 m³, what is its height?

61 Which ones are not correctly simplified?

a. $2x^{-5} = \frac{2}{x^5}$

b. $\frac{(3x)^0}{5^0} = \frac{1}{5}$

c. $(x^5)^2 = x^7$

62 Multiply: $(5a + 2b)(ab - 3)$

63 If Maria can download 12 songs in 15 minutes and her friend Abby can download 12 songs in 20 minutes, how many songs can they get (between the two of them) in two hours?

64 Express $\frac{1}{16}$ using negative exponents.

○ 2^{-4} ○ 16^{-2}

○ $\frac{1}{2^{-4}}$ ○ (-4^2)

65 Find m∠BCA in the figure below.

A: x
B: 3x-22
C: x+2

Answer Key

TASK 1a (pg 14)
1. rational, real, integers
2. a. 7; b. –12; c. 11
3. Francis
4. a. $\frac{2}{3}$; b. $\frac{1}{8}$; c. (–1); d. $\frac{1}{4}$; e. 1; f. ($-\frac{1}{6}$)
5. b, c, f, and h

TASK 1b (pg 15)
1. prime
2. 4^{-3}; 2.4545; 0.062; $\frac{3}{4}$; –14; 9^2; 6.2×10^3; 3.16
3. c should read |12| > |–7|; d should read |2| + |–12| = 14
4. a. $\frac{7}{4}$ or $1\frac{3}{4}$; b. $\frac{2}{x}$; c. $\frac{1}{(-5)}$; d. $\frac{1}{15}$; e. $\frac{4}{3}$; f. $\frac{1}{\sqrt{6}}$
5. a, b, d, f

TASK 2a (pg 16)
1. Monday
2. $\sqrt{144} = 2(2^8)$
3. .625
4. c
5. 640%, 6.4×10^{-1}, -2^5, $\sqrt[3]{64,000}$

TASK 2b (pg 17)
1. a. 34; b. $\frac{2}{3}$
2. 0.9919 < 0.9909
3. 0.812 or .812
4. b
5. Color these teeth: a. 13; b. 27; c. 11; d. 26; e. 18; f. 4

TASK 3a (pg 18)
1. d
2. n(3 + 9) = 3n + 9n
3. (3 • 7) + 0 = 21
4. associative property for multiplication
5. Properties used (in order): additive identity; additive inverse; multiplicative inverse

TASK 3b (pg 19)
1. b
2. 10(6 – 4x + 12y) = 60 – 40x + 120y
3. 55 • 1 = 55
4. reciprocal property
5. Properties used (in order): distributive; additive inverse; additive inverse; multiplicative inverse

TASK 4a (pg 20)
1. Multiply the elements inside the parentheses.
2. 50
3. 1st: combine –4 and –3 inside the parentheses to get –7;
   2nd: multiply –1 and –7 to get 7;
   last: add 24 and 36
4. b
5. A. a = 20; b = 30; B. expression a

TASK 4b (pg 21)
1. Find the square of 80.
2. add –32 and 19
3. Multiply inside the parentheses 2 x 9; subtract inside the parentheses 18 – 4; add 9 + 14.

4. c
5. Monica

TASK 5a (pg 22)
1. $590
2. –18
3. b, d
4. D
5. A: d; B: 492

TASK 5b (pg 23)
1. sum = 0
2. the last two: –x – x and –x(x)
3. c
4. B
5. 350 – (–45) = 395 ft difference

TASK 6a (pg 24)
1. a. 4; b. d
2. two (6n and n)
3. a. m; b. p; c. p; d. b; e. m; f. b
4. b, c, and d
5. (the first expression) 2(d + m) + 4b + c

TASK 6b (pg 25)
1. a. 5; b. bw
2. two: 2y and 7y
3. the second one: $ab^2 - b^2 + a + b$
4. a. in; b. ex; c. eq; d. in
5. Answers will vary. Examples:
   a. $-6d + ab - cd^2$
   b. $a^2b - a^3$
   c. $6bc - 3c + 5c + a^3 - 7c$

TASK 7a (pg 26)
1. 3(m + 2)
2. b
3. x(x + 7)
4. Written expressions may vary somewhat: the sum of four times a number (a) and two less another number (b)
5. Answers may vary: $\frac{(m + m^2 + 18)}{2}$

TASK 7b (pg 27)
1. $868 - n + \frac{1}{3}n$
2. a
3. b^3d^2
4. Written expressions may vary somewhat: half of nine times the difference between a number (x) and the square of another number (y)
5. b

TASK 8a (pg 28)
1. $g^2 + 14m + 5h + 11s + 2h^2$ (Order of the elements may vary.)
2. In the simplifications, order of the elements may vary.
   a. $b^2 - 8b + 48$; b. 24d; c. p^2
3. first two expressions on the left
4. a. 60 mph; b. 4,000; c. 27
5. 1. B > A; 2. A > B; 3. N; 4. B > A

TASK 8b (pg 29)
1. 30s

2. In the simplifications, order of the elements may vary.
   a. 1; b. $8y - 5y^2 + 48$; c. $-5ab^3$
3. a. 7 in; b. 132 lb; c. 1,700 mi; d. 9,000 ft
4. top right : $w(12 + w - 2) = w^2 + 10w$
5. Order is C (–70), D (–15), A (–14), E (–6), B (0)

TASK 9a (pg 30)
1. Sirius 8.6; Barnard's 6; Proxima Centauri 4.2
2. b
3. 1,989,100,000,000,000,000,000,000,000,000
4. 3^{-2}
5. A. $\frac{1}{64}$; B. 13; C. 1; D. $\sqrt[4]{y^3}$; E. –12, $\frac{1}{12^{-1}}$

TASK 9b (pg 31)
1. a. 9.3×10^7; b. 1.4×10^6; c. 5.8×10^3; d. 4.5×10^9
2. the third group
3. the first three expressions
4. a. 15; b. 6; c. 2; d. –4; e. $1\frac{3}{4}$; f. $\frac{2}{5}$
5. A. Circle all examples.
   B. Circle $5\sqrt{144} = 60$ and $8^0 = 1$.

TASK 10a (pg 32)
1. 3,350 m
2. a, b, c, e
3. c, d, a, b
4. 4.6×10^5
5. A. 2002; B. 2007; C. 1971; D. 1996

TASK 10b (pg 33)
1. 2008 – 25 = 1983
2. b, c
3. e, d, b, c, a
4. 3.7×10^5
5. a. 4,190 ft; b. 165 m; c. 23,000 yrs; d. 61

TASK 11a (pg 34)
1. a. 96; b. 72; c. 144
2. 2, 3, 6, 7, 14
3. b
4. 236; (LCM = 240, GCF = 4)
5. Fly: can get caught by numbers:

A	2,187			40,545	972
B	2,187	70, 320		40,545	972
C		70,320			972
D		70,320	1,256		
E		70,320	1,256		972

TASK 11b (pg 35)
1. a. 3; b. one (2007)
2. 630
3. 2, 3, 4, 5, 6, 8, 10, 12, 15, 20, 24, 30, 40, 60, 120
4. 87; (LCM = 90, GCF = 3)
5. 1,080

TASK 12a (pg 36)
1. $\frac{1}{9} \cdot 230 = 25\frac{5}{9}$
2. 3.645
3. B > A
4. a, b, c, f
5. a. 30 lbs; b. 2,850

TASK 12b (pg 37)
1. a. 0.6 in^2; b. 5.06 in^2
2. .00252
3. A > B
4. a. $\frac{3ac}{2b}$; b. $14\frac{3}{8}$; c. $\frac{1}{2}$
5. A, C, D, E

TASK 13a (pg 38)
1. 13.33%
2. 20
3. a. 85%; b. 34; c. 625; d. 25%
4. $28
5. a. B; b. A; c. N; d. D; e. C; f. N

TASK 13b (pg 39)
1. 82%
2. 433.3%
3. 200%
4. a. 65%; b. 162; c. 500; d. 116%
5. a. cherry bombs; b. 28.6%;
   c. 5.7%; d. sparklers

TASK 14a (pg 40)
1. 2, 3, y, n
2. 6a
3. r^2
4. Answers will vary. Some possibilities:
   (–4x) (6x^3); (12x^2) (–2x^2); (–x^3) (24x)
5. A, B, C

TASK 14b (pg 41)
1. 2
2. 4xy
3. 9y^2, z^2, q
4. Answers will vary. Some possibilities:
   (36ab)(2ab^4); (8a)(9ab^5); (ab^3)(72ab^2)
5. B, E

TASK 15a (pg 42)
1. b
2. yes
3. b
4. Equations may vary somewhat. Example:
   1,000 = 25t + 25(t – 2); t = 21
5. c

TASK 15b (pg 43)
1. c
2. Equations may vary somewhat. Example:
   x + 2(x – 840) = 2,040; x = 1,240
3. b
4. no
5. A. a (239); B. d (263); C. 2,630

TASK 16a (pg 44)
1. t = 15
2. 16
3. a, c
4. Equations may vary somewhat. Example:
   12w = 9 (w = 0.5 oz)
5. 1. B > A;   2. A > B;   3. B > A

TASK 16b (pg 45)
1. 26 in
2. 1
3. b, c
4. Equations may vary somewhat. Example:
   50r = 1,500 (r = 30)
5. A. c; B. 12 minutes

TASK 17a (pg 46)
1. Equations may vary somewhat. Example:
   6d = 252; d = 42 ft
2. 112
3. b = –15
4. –14
5. Tyler: 40   Emily: 20   Gabe: 28
   James: 169   Charlene: 67   Maria: 88
   A. Emily and Tyler
   B. Emily and Maria

TASK 17b (pg 47)
1. Equations may vary somewhat.
   $\frac{1}{5}$x = 68 (x = 340)
2. –16
3. n = –6
4. –4.5
5. Benjamin: 44; Dionne: 256; Jasmine: 12;
   Mari: 3; Anna: 32

TASK 18a (pg 48)
1. c. x = 3 ft
2. B > A (A: d = –4 and B: c = –2)
3. p = 4
4. 4 and 3
5. A. Choose equation a to find x = 12
   B. 28 surfers total
   C. 16

TASK 18b (pg 49)
1. e. w = 24
2. CIRCLE: A > B
3. m = (–6)
4. A. c; B. b
5. A. Angela = 7; Brad = 14; Charlie = 42;
   B. Brad will be $\frac{3}{7}$ Charlie's age.   OR
   Charlie will be $2\frac{1}{3}$ times Brad's age.

TASK 19a (pg 50)
1. 18 inches
2. no (sum is $7\frac{1}{2}$)
3. a
4. a. x = $\frac{1}{4}$; b. n = $\frac{1}{2}$; c. p = $\frac{3}{4}$; d = 1
   Each solution is $\frac{1}{4}$ greater than the
   previous solution.
5. Equations may vary. p – $\frac{1}{6}$p – $\frac{2}{6}$p – $\frac{2}{5}$
   p($\frac{1}{6}$p – $\frac{2}{6}$p) = $28\frac{4}{5}$;
   a. 96; b. 16; c. 32; d. $19\frac{1}{5}$

TASK 19b (pg 51)
1. 3.7 in
2. yes (sum is $8\frac{1}{3}$)
3. x = 10
4. a. v = (–2)   b. w = (–4)
   c. y = (–6)   d. z = (–8)
   Each solution is 2 less than
   the previous solution
5. A. 4 ft; B. 6 ft; C. $10\frac{1}{2}$ ft

TASK 20a (pg 52)
1. a; x = 4
2. B
3. y = 9
4. 95
5. a. 180,000; b. 1.6 x 10^3

TASK 20b (pg 53)
1. t = 33 ft
2. A and B
3. x = 2
4. 0
5. a. (4.8 x 10^5 or 480,000) x = 600 lb
   b. 1,000 sq ft ^{3}; 10 x 10 x 10 ft

TASK 21a (pg 54)
1. c and e; rate = 70 mph
2. t = 12 hr
3. a. Train A; b. 80 miles
4. 300
5. a. 10:59 P.M. (CST) Saturday
   b. 1,656 miles

TASK 21b (pg 55)
1. 82(t – 5) = 1,230;
   traveling time = 20 hours
2. r = 48 mph
3. a. the car; b. 275 miles
4. 30
5. a. 60 mph; b. 66 mph

TASK 22a (pg 56)
1. c; n = 27
2. a. x = 7; b. x = 4; c. x = 60
3. $\frac{24}{6}$ and $\frac{96}{60}$
4. a. $\frac{7}{61}$; b. $\frac{2b}{5}$; c. $\frac{2y}{7}$
5. 6 mi

TASK 22b (pg 57)
1. c
2. a. x = 13; b. x = 75; c. x = 8
3. $\frac{4}{11}$
4. a. $\frac{1}{36}$; b. $\frac{2d^3f}{7}$; c. 2z
5. a. 24 dogs; b. Day 25; c. 140

TASK 23a (pg 58)
1. $\frac{1}{36}$ ($\frac{1}{6}$ x $\frac{1}{6}$)
2. $\frac{3}{8}$
3. 6:8
4. 30
5. a. $\frac{13}{18}$; b. $\frac{25}{89}$; c. $\frac{1}{89}$

TASK 23b (pg 59)
1. $\frac{1}{4}$
2. $\frac{5}{8}$
3. 11:2
4. 120
5. a. $\frac{5}{18}$; b. $\frac{10}{153}$; c. $\frac{4}{17}$

TASK 24a (pg 60)
1. 2x + 5 ≤ (–3)
2. a
3. x > 25

I've Got It!—Pre-Algebra Skills
Copyright ©2008 by Incentive Publications, Inc., Nashville, TN.

4.
5. Boat is C

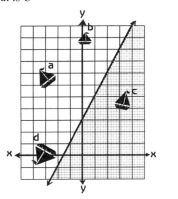

TASK 24b (pg 61)
1. $3x - (-4) > 22$
2. $b \geq 8$
3. b
4.
5. They are on Island D.

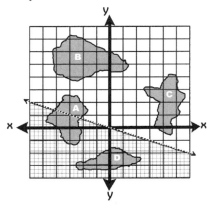

TASK 25a (pg 62)
1. $c = 3$; $b = 6$
2. a. $y = 5$; b. $n = 4$ so $b > a$
3. $\frac{1}{8} x^3 y^5$
4. a. $c = 5$; b. $c = 45$
5. a. 6
   b. It will increase by 8 times.
   c. 40; Jen is 2 (talk balloon)

TASK 25b (pg 63)
1. $t = 24$; $a = 12$
2. $n = -2$ and $f = -5$, so $n > f$
3. $\frac{5}{8} wx^2$
4. a. $g = 3$; b. $g = 12$
5. a. 50
   b. It will decrease.
   c. Nat could be 2 and Pat could be 4. OR Nat could be 5 and Pat could be 2.

TASK 26a (pg 64)
1. 10 in
2. 28 cm
3. 135°
4. 140°
5. a. one square = 7 x 7 in
   b. 35 in

TASK 26b (pg 65)
1. none of these
2. 45 in
3. 120°
4. 140°
5. a. Each square = 4 x 4 in; b. 42 in

TASK 27a (pg 66)
1. A
2. $d = 8$ cm
3. CIRCLE: cone
4. 228 cm³
5. a. orange – 12 bottles; b. pink – 2 bottles

TASK 27b (pg 67)
1. D
2. $B = 1,200$ ft²
3. CIRCLE: prism (B)
4. 38 m³
5. a. 1,708.16 in²; b. No. The diameter of the inside will be smaller by 0.4 in.

TASK 28a (pg 68)
1. 47°
2. 26 cm
3. a
4. c
5. 0.4 mile

TASK 28b (pg 69)
1. 60°
2. 32.7
3. 17.5
4. b
5. 12 minutes

TASK 29a (pg 70)
1. none
2. (0, –4)
3. (7, 0)
4. a. fish; b. swim fin; c. fish; d. treasure chest
5. Check drawings to see that items are placed accurately.

TASK 29b (pg 71)
1. two: (–20, 4) and (–18, 4)
2. (4, –6)
3. (7, 2)
4. a. bubble; b. anchor; d. hat; d. bubble
5. Check drawings to see that items are placed accurately.

TASK 30a (pg 72)
1. A
2. Check drawings for accuracy.
3. (–8, 10)
4. (–6, –5)
5. yes

TASK 30b (pg 73)
1. A
2. Check drawings for accuracy.
3. (4, –2)
4. (5, 4)
5. No; he did not rotate the figure far enough.

TASK 31a (pg 74)
1. CIRCLE: a, c, e
2. b
3. yes, an absolute value function
4. {–3, –1, 0, 3, 4}
5. This is a function. There are two ways to tell.
   1) For any value of x, there is only one value of y.
   2) The graph passes the vertical line test. Examine table and graph for accuracy.

y = 2x - 1		
x	y	(x, y)
-2	-5	(-2, -5)
-1	-3	(-1, -3)
0	-1	(0, -1)
1	1	(1, 1)
2	3	(2, 3)

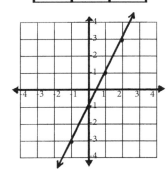

TASK 31b (pg 75)
1. CIRCLE: a, b, c, d, e
2. b
3. yes
4. {–7, –5, –4, –1, 0}
5. This is a function. There are two ways to tell.
   1) For any value of x, there is only one value of y.
   2) The graph passes the vertical line test. Examine table and graph for accuracy.

y + 1 = 3x		
x	y	(x, y)
-2	-7	(-2, -7)
-1	-4	(-1, -4)
0	-1	(0, -1)
1	2	(1, 2)
2	5	(2, 5)

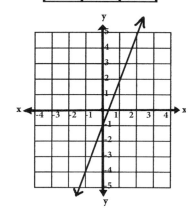

TASK 32a (pg 76)
1. A, C, D
2. C; slope = 1
3. B
4. a. 6; b. 6
5. Slope intercept form is: y = x + 1

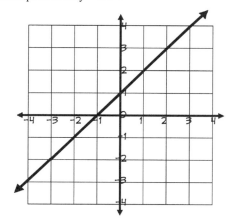

TASK 32b (pg 77)
1. B, C, E
2. B; 1
3. neither
4. a. 4; b. 4
5. Slope-intercept form is: y = 2x – 3

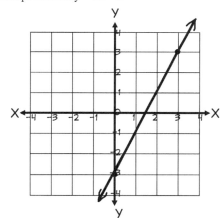

TASK 33a (pg 78)
1. negative
2. a. 1; b. $-\frac{3}{4}$; c. $\frac{4}{5}$; d. 0
3. $\frac{1}{7}$
4. x + 2y = –19
5. a. –2; b. $-\frac{2}{3}$; c. Skier B

TASK 33b (pg 79)
1. Derek
2. a. $\frac{1}{5}$; b. 4; c. –1; d. 1
3. –3
4. a. $(-\frac{5}{7})$; b. $-\frac{11}{7}$ or –1.57
5. a. Snowboarder Y; b. 5; c. –3

TASK 34a (pg 80)
1. CIRCLE: A and B
2. 9rs
3. A. c; B. none of these
4. $12x^2y + 3x^3y - 24y - 6xy$ (Terms may be in a different order.)
5. d

TASK 34b (pg 81)
1. CIRCLE: A. $15p - 5pq + 3p + q^2$; C. $10xy^2 - x$
2. $3x^3 + 11y - 12$
3. A. a; B. b
4. $7a^4b^4 + 30a^2b^2 - 25$
5. f

TASK 35a (pg 82)
1. $x + 6 = 1\frac{3}{8}x$; x = 16 (x is Tyler's age); Trent is 22.
2. b
3. t = 20 ÷ (5 – 1); t = 5 hours
4. 450% increase
5. a. 10 feet; b. 540 ft^2

TASK 35b (pg 83)
1. x + 4 = 2x – 9; x = 13 (x is Charlie's age); Derek's age is 15.
2. g
3. $\frac{78}{3} = \frac{234}{x}$; x = 18 weeks
4. $\frac{1}{40}$
5. a. canoe B; b. $\frac{1}{7}$; c. $-\frac{6}{5}$ or $-1\frac{1}{5}$

Putting It All Together (pgs 86–91)

1. N	14. B	27. 75	40. (–7, 4)	53. a
2. B	15. A	28. d	41. –4	54. 10
3. B	16. B	29. 2 m	42. 1.38 x 10^{-1}	55. 80
4. E	17. N	30. 6	43. 4 hours	56. $\frac{5}{2}$
5. A	18. B	31. paw print	44. 0.47	57. no
6. B	19. N	32. 2	45. $-6x^2 - 9xy - 27x$	58. (3, –2)
7. E	20. A	33. 11	46. yes	59. yes
8. A	21. $\frac{1}{46}$	34. 23rd	47. x ≤ –6	60. 6 m
9. B	22. 20	35. a	48. a	61. b and c
10. A	23. b	36. a, d	49. –140.7	62. $5a^2b - 15a + 2ab^2 - 6b$
11. E	24. yes	37. 234	50. no	63. 168
12. A	25. a, b	38. 15 in	51. 750,000	64. 2^{-4}
13. E	26. 2a	39. –21	52. 36%	65. 42°